NEW DIRECTIONS FOR INSTITUTIONAL RESEARCH

J. Fredericks Volkwein, *State University of New York at Albany*
EDITOR-IN-CHIEF

Larry H. Litten, *Consortium on Financing Higher Education,
Cambridge, Massachusetts*
ASSOCIATE EDITOR

Faculty Teaching and Research: Is There a Conflict?

John M. Braxton
Vanderbilt University

EDITOR

Number 90, Summer 1996

JOSSEY-BASS PUBLISHERS
San Francisco

FACULTY TEACHING AND RESEARCH: IS THERE A CONFLICT?
John M. Braxton (ed.)
New Directions for Institutional Research, no. 90
Volume XVIII, Number 2
J. Fredericks Volkwein, Editor-in-Chief

Microfilm copies of issues and articles are available in 16mm and 35mm, as well as microfiche in 105mm, through University Microfilms Inc., 300 North Zeeb Road, Ann Arbor, Michigan 48106-1346.

ISSN 0271-0579   ISBN 0-7879-9898-2

NEW DIRECTIONS FOR INSTITUTIONAL RESEARCH is part of The Jossey-Bass Higher and Adult Education Series and is published quarterly by Jossey-Bass Inc., Publishers, 350 Sansome Street, San Francisco, California 94104-1342 (publication number USPS 098-830). Periodicals postage paid at San Francisco, California, and at additional mailing offices. POST-MASTER: Send address changes to New Directions for Institutional Research, Jossey-Bass Inc., Publishers, 350 Sansome Street, San Francisco, California 94104-1342.

SUBSCRIPTIONS for 1996 cost $50.00 for individuals and $72.00 for institutions, agencies, and libraries.

EDITORIAL CORRESPONDENCE should be sent to J. Fredericks Volkwein, Institutional Research, Administration 241, State University of New York at Albany, Albany, NY 12222.

Photograph of the library by Michael Graves at San Juan Capistrano by Chad Slattery © 1984. All rights reserved.

Manufactured in the United States of America on Lyons Falls Pathfinder Tradebook. This paper is acid-free and 100 percent totally chlorine-free.

Contents

EDITOR'S NOTES   1
John M. Braxton

1. Contrasting Perspectives on the Relationship Between Teaching   5
and Research
John M. Braxton
Empirical backing for the Null, Complementarity, and Conflict perspectives
on the relationship between research activity and overall instructor effectiveness is appraised.

2. Teaching Norms and Publication Productivity   15
Anna V. Shaw Sullivan
The influence of faculty research activity on the espousal of four norms of
undergraduate college teaching is examined.

3. Research Activity and the Support of Undergraduate Education   23
Nathaniel J. Bray, John M. Braxton, John C. Smart
The hypothesis that research activity fosters faculty attitudes that are unsup-
portive of improving undergraduate education is tested.

4. The Research Versus Teaching Debate: Untangling the   31
Relationships
Deborah Olsen, Ada Simmons
The relationship between faculty research activity and the choice of instruc-
tional practices favoring personal efficiency over instructional effectiveness
and the enactment of good practices of undergraduate education is assessed.

5. Faculty Productivity and the Complexity of Student Exam   41
Questions
Robert M. Johnson, Jr.
The relationship between the rigor of course examination questions and
faculty research activity is pursued.

6. Triangulating the Relationships Among Publication Productivity,   49
Teaching Effectiveness, and Student Achievement
Michael Gavlick
A model positing a relationship between faculty research activity, instruc-
tor behaviors, and student achievement is advanced.

7. Institutional and Departmental Cultures: The Relationship   57
Between Teaching and Research
Ann E. Austin
The influence of institutional and departmental cultures on the relationship
between teaching and research is discussed, and suggestions for nurturing
a positive relationship between them are made.

8. Framing the Public Policy Debate on Faculty: What Is the Role   67
of Research?
Meredith Jane Ludwig
The public debate on the activities of faculty is discussed, and approaches
for research on these activities are offered.

9. Public Trust, Research Activity, and the Ideal of Service to   79
Students as Clients of Teaching
John M. Braxton, Joseph B. Berger
Using the empirical evidence presented in this volume, the question of
whether faculty research activity hinders meeting the needs of students as
"clients of teaching" is addressed.

INDEX   93

EDITOR'S NOTES

In this volume of *New Directions for Institutional Research*, the authors examine the tension between the teaching and research activities of college and university faculty. Examining the relationship between teaching and research is a long-standing and fundamental part of the study of college and university faculty. The dynamics of this relationship generate interest among public policy makers and parents. Many members of the lay public assert that teaching undergraduate students is the faculty's most important responsibility (Ewell, 1994). Consequently, the public often views faculty research activity as an intrusion on teaching undergraduate students (Volkwein and Carbone, 1994).

Scholars such as Massy and Zemsky (1994) echo this perspective. They argue that faculty members who are heavily involved in research increase their use of discretionary time to do research at the expense of teaching. To them, time is zero sum, and time devoted to research takes time away from teaching. Time spent on teaching also reduces the publication productivity of faculty (Fox, 1992).

However, viewing teaching as simply an expenditure of time belies the complexity of this professorial role. Facets of the teaching role include classroom performance, teaching preparations, the influence of teaching behaviors on student learning, faculty goals for undergraduate education, faculty attitudes and behaviors concerning interactions with students, pedagogical practices, course assessment activities, norms delineating inappropriate teaching behaviors, and adherence to good teaching practices.

In the first six chapters of this *New Directions for Institutional Research* volume, the authors examine the relationship between research activity and these various facets of performing the teaching role. In the first chapter, I assess the extent of support for three contrasting perspectives on the relationship between teaching and research: Null, Conflict, and Complementarity. I appraise the support for each of these contrasting perspectives using extant research on the relationship between faculty research activity and student ratings of these faculty members' overall instructional effectiveness. I conclude that the Conflict perspective garners little or no support, whereas both the Null and the Complementarity perspectives receive moderate backing.

In the second chapter, Anna V. Shaw Sullivan looks at the relationship between research activity and the subscription to four undergraduate teaching norms. These four norms proscribe a set of four inappropriate behaviors that are injurious to the welfare of students—the clients of teaching performance.

Next, Nathaniel J. Bray, John M. Braxton, and John C. Smart consider the relationship between research activity and faculty attitudes toward the goals for undergraduate education and toward being accessible to students. Both of these attitudes connect directly to needed improvements in undergraduate education:

curricular reform (Association of American Colleges, 1985) and the encouragement of faculty and student interactions (Chickering and Gamson, 1987).

In the fourth chapter, Deborah Olsen and Ada Simmons focus on whether faculty who are heavily involved in research choose pedagogical practices that are personally efficient over those that are instructionally effective. They also look at whether research activity affects faculty enactment of Chickering and Gamson's (1987) principles of good teaching practice.

Robert M. Johnson, Jr., in the fifth chapter, concentrates on the assessment practices that faculty use in their courses and the relationship of these practices to faculty involvement in research. Johnson identifies an association between the level of faculty research activity and the rigor of course examination questions.

Next, Michael Gavlick finds a possible link between research activity and student knowledge acquisition in courses. The model Gavlick posits in this sixth chapter triangulates meta-analyses conducted by Feldman (1987) on the relationship between teaching and research, and by Cohen (1981) on the correlation between instructor behaviors and student course achievement.

In the remaining three chapters, the authors consider the implications of the relationship between teaching and research for public policy and institutional practice. In the seventh chapter, Ann E. Austin describes departmental and institutional cultures and their influence on the relationship between teaching and research. She also offers suggestions for nurturing cultures in which both teaching and research are valued.

Meredith Jane Ludwig argues in Chapter Eight that public policy makers are not interested in the relationship between teaching and research. Instead, they want to know what faculty do with their time. In this chapter, Ludwig suggests the approaches to conducting research that are desired by public policy makers.

In the last chapter, Joseph B. Berger and I summarize the volume within the context of public trust and faculty service to clients. Violations of the public's trust in faculty to follow the ideal of service to students leads public policy makers to question the work activities of faculty. We appraise the relationship between research and various dimensions of teaching, and we generally find that research activity does not adversely affect faculty adherence to the ideal of service. We also suggest implications for practice and future research derived from this assessment.

Each of the chapters in this volume articulates implications for practice. In some chapters, the authors make recommendations for further research by institutional researchers and other scholars. As a consequence, public policy makers, college and university presidents, academic affairs officers, institutional researchers, scholars of higher education, and individual faculty members should find this volume useful.

The relationship between teaching and research is complex. The chapters of this volume demonstrate this complexity and increase our understanding of it. Such an understanding is essential to the enhancement of both teaching and research. Moreover, the restoration of public trust in faculty depends on such fine-grained understanding. Without public trust, faculty autonomy and financial support for higher education will suffer.

John M. Braxton
Editor

References

Association of American Colleges. *Integrity in the College Curriculum: A Report to the Academic Community*. Washington, D.C.: Association of American Colleges, 1985.

Chickering, A. W., and Gamson, Z. E. "Seven Principles for Good Practice in Undergraduate Education." *AAHE Bulletin*, 1987, *39*, 3–7.

Cohen, P. A. "Student Ratings of Instruction and Student Achievement: A Meta-Analysis of Multisection Validity Studies." *Review of Educational Research*, 1981, *51*, (3), 281–309.

Ewell, P. T. "The Neglected Art of Collective Responsibility: Restoring Our Links with Society." Commissioned paper for the American Association of Higher Education Forum on Faculty Roles and Rewards Second National Conference, New Orleans, January 1994.

Feldman, K. A. "Research Productivity and Scholarly Accomplishment of College Teachers as Related to Their Instructional Effectiveness: A Review and Exploration." *Research in Higher Education*, 1987, *26*, 227–98.

Fox, M. F. "Research, Teaching, and Publication Productivity: Mutuality Versus Competition in Academia." *Sociology of Education*, 1992, *65*, 293–305.

Massy, W. F., and Zemsky, R. "Faculty Discretionary Time: Departments and the 'Academic Ratchet.'" *Journal of Higher Education*, 1994, *65*, 1–22.

Volkwein, F. J., and Carbone, D. A. "The Impact of Departmental Research and Teaching Climates on Undergraduate Growth and Satisfaction." *Journal of Higher Education*, 1994, *65*, 147–167.

JOHN M. BRAXTON is associate professor of education in the Department of Educational Leadership, Peabody College, Vanderbilt University in Nashville, Tennessee. His research focuses on the sociology of the academic profession, with an emphasis on faculty role performance and professional self-regulation of research and teaching.

Empirical support for three contrasting perspectives on the relationship between teaching and research—Null, Conflict, and Complementarity—is assessed. Both the Null and Complementarity perspectives receive modest affirmation, whereas the Conflict perspective garners scant support.

Contrasting Perspectives on the Relationship Between Teaching and Research

John M. Braxton

In the current climate of accountability, the research activities of university faculty receive public scrutiny and criticism both from members of the academy and the lay public. Such members of the academy as Kerr (1963), Veysey (1965), and Clark (1987) hold that research and teaching conflict and that undergraduate education suffers as a result. Boyer (1990) gives form to this conflict in *Scholarship Reconsidered: Priorities of the Professoriate*. He asserts that research activity competes with teaching obligations for time and content. To accommodate research activity, faculty teaching loads are reduced, and teaching assistants are assigned to large undergraduate courses (Boyer, 1990). Thus, the perception emerges that student needs are ignored because faculty pursue their own scholarly interests.

This perception runs contrary to the expectations of the lay public—parents, legislators, students, and members of boards of trustees. The public expects faculty members to concentrate more of their efforts on teaching undergraduates than on their scholarly and research activities (Volkwein and Carbone, 1994). This expectation led to the scrutiny of faculty teaching loads in five states (Cage, 1991).

Moreover, Massy and Zemsky (1994) contend that colleges and universities are unable to control costs and to set institutional priorities because of the discretionary time faculty have available to them. Reduced teaching loads create such discretionary time. The "academic ratchet" is the term Massy and Zemsky use to describe increments in the use of discretionary time at the expense of teaching.

These authors suggest that the roles of teaching and research conflict with one another (Fox, 1992). In other words, the two roles are negatively related. However, two alternative perspectives compete with this view. One perspective holds that teaching and research are complementary (Faia, 1976; Fox, 1992) and form an integrated core of activities for the academic profession (Parsons and Platt, 1973; Shils, 1983). The other perspective contends that there is no relationship between teaching and research (Harry and Goldner, 1972; Linsky and Straus, 1975; Finkelstein, 1984).

The Contrasting Perspectives

The three perspectives—Null, Conflict, and Complementarity—are more fully described as follows.

Null. This perspective posits that there is no relationship between teaching and research; the roles are independent of one another (Finkelstein, 1984) and do not detract from one another (Linsky and Straus, 1975). Thus, the null relationship may be the inverse of complementarity. More specifically, teaching and research may be clearly set apart by general ability, professional goals, and values. Also, there may be a lack of correspondence between teaching and research specializations. Moreover, these two roles may not be mutually reinforcing.

Conflict. There are several variations of the position that a negative relationship exists between teaching and research. One is that the roles of teaching and research conflict because they carry different expectations and different obligations (Fox, 1992). Another variation is the assertion that the allocation of time sums to zero. Because productive scholars spend more time in research, they spend less time in teaching. Consequently, the quality of teaching is adversely affected by the lesser amount of time spent in teaching activities (Finkelstein, 1984). A third variant is that teaching and research require different abilities and personality traits (Linsky and Straus, 1975; Finkelstein, 1984).

Complementarity. Complementarity refers to the extent to which the roles of teaching and research are similar (Faia, 1976). There are several dimensions on which teaching and research may share similarities. General ability is one such dimension. Teaching and research require the same general ability in the enactment of these two roles (Linsky and Straus, 1975; Finkelstein, 1984). Because the academic profession's basic goal of "furthering knowledge" can be realized through both research and teaching, professional goals represents another dimension on which similarity may exist (Faia, 1976).

Values are another point of possible similarity (Parsons and Platt, 1973; Shils, 1983; Fox, 1992). Holding cognitive rationality as a value, for example, suggests favoring an integration of the roles of teaching and research (Parsons and Platt, 1968). Cognitive rationality is the comprehension and solution of intellectual problems in rational terms (Platt, Parsons, and Kirshtein, 1976); this value pattern manifests itself in both teaching and research (Braxton, 1983).

Role complementarity can also exist if teaching and research are carried out in the same areas of specialization within an academic discipline (Faia, 1976).

Teaching and research may also be positively related because these roles are mutually reinforcing. Linsky and Straus (1975) postulate that there is a spill-over effect into teaching from doing research, and vice versa. For example, excitement generated by engagement in research may be communicated to students during the course of instruction. Likewise, stimulating teaching could generate student questions that might suggest topics for research. Finkelstein (1984) suggests another aspect of the spill-over effect. He contends that because productive scholars keep up with and make advances in their disciplines, they are more likely to exhibit a higher degree of interest and expertise in their teaching, and their performance is enhanced.

A fundamental question is raised by the existence of these three contrasting perspectives: To what extent are they supported by empirical research? Although three reviews of empirical research have been conducted on the relationship between teaching and research (Faia, 1976; Finkelstein, 1984; Feldman, 1987), Feldman's (1987) meta-analysis is the most recent and most comprehensive. From the twenty-nine studies reviewed, he calculated an average correlation of +.12 ($p < .001$) between research productivity and student assessments of teaching effectiveness.[1] Thus, Feldman found some support for complementarity between teaching and research.

This method of averaging the correlations obtained from the twenty-nine studies is appropriate for deriving an aggregated measure of association between teaching and research. However, the method does not permit the simultaneous appraisal of the three contrasting perspectives because it masks variation in findings among the individual studies. The weak overall correlation ($r = .12$, $p < .001$) found by Feldman reinforces this argument, as it suggests considerable variation among individual studies. Thus, we want the opportunity to gain what Platt (1964) calls "strong inference" through the simultaneous testing of contrasting positions.

Consequently, in this chapter I will use a technique that permits the simultaneous assessment of support for each of the three contrasting perspectives: the "box score," or the "vote-counting" method (Light and Smith, 1971).

This approach entails tallying the proportion of studies that support each of the three contrasting perspectives. This method was applied to thirty studies: the twenty-nine studies used by Feldman to calculate an average r (1987) and one additional study (Voeks, 1962) that Feldman reviewed but did not include in his calculation. These thirty studies focus on the relationship between research productivity and student appraisals of teaching effectiveness. The method will allow me to answer the question, To what extent are the contrasting perspectives sustained by research?

I will also address one additional question: Does the extent of support for the three perspectives vary across different types of colleges and universities? Support may vary among different types of colleges and universities because of variations within the institutions in the amount of emphasis placed on teaching and research.

Method of Allocating Support and Assessing Strength

I have used the following criteria to categorize each study according to the perspective supported. Studies reporting a statistically significant average correlation between teaching and research of +.10 or higher support the Complementarity perspective. Studies indicating a statistically reliable average correlation between teaching and research of -.10 or lower affirm the Conflict perspective. Studies reporting a statistically significant average correlation between -.09 and +.09 confirm the Null perspective.[2] Studies reporting statistically nonsignificant average correlations also support the Null perspective.[3]

I assess the extent of support for each perspective by using the percentage of studies that sustain a given perspective. "Strong" support is noted when 66 percent or more of the total number of studies reviewed affirm a given perspective. "Modest" or "moderate" support is noted if between 34 and 65 percent of the studies reviewed confirm a given perspective. If 33 percent or fewer of the total number of studies used was categorized as supporting a given perspective, I attribute weak support to this perspective.

Overall Support. Table 1.1 exhibits studies backing each of the three contrasting perspectives. Both the Complementarity perspective (eleven of thirty studies) and the Null perspective (eighteen of thirty studies) receive moderate support. The Conflict perspective receives weak support, given that only one of the thirty studies reviewed sustains this perspective.

Support by Institutional Type. Because Feldman (1987) provided the names of the institutions he reviewed, it is possible to classify them according to their Carnegie Classification Category (1987).[4] Table 1.2 shows that the Null perspective receives strong affirmation in research universities. However, both the Null and the Complementarity perspectives garner modest backing in each of the remaining four categories of colleges and universities: doctoral-granting universities, comprehensive universities and colleges, liberal arts colleges, and unspecified types of collegiate institutions.

Conclusions and Implications

We can draw two conclusions from our appraisal of support for each of the three contrasting perspectives. First, research does not interfere with teaching effectiveness. This conclusion is particularly salient in research universities in which the Null perspective receives strong confirmation. Moreover, the Conflict perspective has empirical support in only one of thirty studies. Second, a systematic relationship between teaching and research role performance does not exist across different types of colleges and universities. This conclusion stems from the modest support provided both the Null and the Complementarity perspectives.

Table 1.1. Overall Support for the Three Contrasting Perspectives on the Relationship Between Teaching and Research

	Perspective Supported	r
Null	Aleamoni and Yimer (1973)	.002[a]
	Bausell and Magoon (1972)	+.07[a]
	Braunstein and Benston (1973)	+.04[a]
	Centra (1983, Study 2)	+.07[a]
	Dent and Lewis (1976)	+.02[a]
	Frey (1978)	+.07[a]
	Friedrich and Michalak (1983)	+.18[a][b]
	Hoyt and Spangler (1976)	+.17[a][b]
	Linsky and Straus (1975)	+.01[a]
	McCullagh and Roy (1975)	+.05[a]
	McDaniel and Feldhusen (1970)	+.04[a]
	Rushton, Murray, and Paunonen (1983)	-.07[a]
	Siegfried and White (1973)	+.03[a]
	Stallings and Singhal (1970, Study 2)	+.11[a][b]
	Stavridis (1972)	+.24[a][b]
	Usher (1966)	+.23[a][b]
	Voeks (1962)	no relationship
	Wood (1978)	-.07[a]
Conflict	Hoffman (1984)	-.25[a]
Complimentarity	Bresler (1968)	+.23[a]
	Centra (1983, Study 1)	+.10[a]
	Clark (1973)	+.30[a]
	Faia (1976)	+.11[a]
	Freedman, Stumpf, and Aguanno (1979)	+.23[a]
	Harry and Goldner (1972)	+.19[a]
	Hicks (1974)	+.25
	Marquardt, McGann, and Jakubauskas (1975)	+.25[a]
	Marsh and Overall (1978)	.14[a]
	Stallings and Singhal (1970, Study 1)	+.26[a]
	Wood and DeLorme (1976)	+.39[a]

Note: Total number of studies = 30.
[a] Derived from Table 1 in Feldman (1987)
[b] Not statistically significant ($p < .05$)

Implications for Researchers and Scholars

The absence of a systematic relationship between teaching and research raises interesting questions for further research. What is the natural state of affairs between these two professional roles? Perhaps, a null relationship represents the natural condition. When complementarity exists, individual faculty characteristics or institutional culture may account for it.

Table 1.2. Support for the Three Contrasting Perspectives by Institutional Type

	RU	DGU	CCU	LAC	NS
Null Perspective	Aleamoni and Yimer	Wood	McCullagh and Roy	Friedrich and Michalak	Centra
	Bausell and Magoon				Dent and Lewis
	Braunstein and Benston				Frey
	Hoyt and Spangler				Linsky and Straus
	McDaniel and Feldhausen				Rushton and others
	Siegfried and White				
	Stallings and Singhal				
	Stavridis				
	Usher				
	Voeks				
Conflict Perspective		Hoffman			
Complementarity Perspective	Marsh and Overall	Bresler	Hicks	Clark	Centra
	Stallings and Singhal				Faia
	Wood and DeLorme				Freedman and others
					Harry and Goldner
					Marquard and others

Note: The studies are exhibited in Table 1.1.
RU = Research Universities, DGU = Doctoral-Granting Universities, CUC = Comprehensive Universities and Colleges, LAC = Liberal Arts Colleges, NS = Nonspecified types of colleges and universities

Individual faculty members may differ in their professional goals and values. A dual orientation toward both roles by some faculty members may account for observed complementarity. The need for cognitive consistency that some academics have may also explain complementarity. Such individuals may highly value cognitive rationality. Because teaching and research both manifest the value pattern of cognitive rationality, a need for cognitive consistency requires high performance in both roles (Braxton, 1983).

When complementarity exists, it may also be due to subtle differences in institutional culture. The equal importance of teaching and research may be a manifestation of the culture of some colleges and universities. Also, some colleges and universities may strive to appoint faculty who are dually oriented toward both teaching and research. Role complementarity would be a likely consequence of such institutional cultures.

Future research should focus on the possible explanations advanced above. Investigations should be conducted in different types of colleges and universities, with special attention to those settings where institutional culture may play a role. The findings from such studies could provide a foundation for institutional policy on faculty personnel issues such as appointment, promotion and tenure, and salaries.

Implications for Administrators

Our conclusions have implications for academic administrators and presidents. First, academic deans, chief academic affairs officers, and presidents can confidently assert that teaching effectiveness and publication activity do not conflict with one another. This message should be delivered to parents and to public policy makers at various levels of government.

Second, the findings of this chapter could be used to frame deliberations by faculty, academic administrators, and presidents on the desired relationship between publication activity and teaching effectiveness at a given college or university. Although many institutions discuss the balance between teaching and research in the reward structure, few institutions debate the relationship these two professional roles should have. Such debate might help colleges and universities to crisply delineate their expectations for the faculty role and relieve the role strain that faculty experience (Bess, 1982; Bayer, 1970).

Some colleges or universities may prefer complementarity between the two professional roles, whereas others may desire a null relationship. Such preferences reflect underlying value differences on the meaning of being an academic within institutions of varying missions and cultures. A preference for complementarity reveals a high value on academics who are dually oriented toward both teaching and research. In contrast, a preference for the null relationship indicates a division among academics of professional duties between teaching and research.

A preference for complementarity requires buttressing institutional policy. Colleges and universities favoring complementarity should encourage the appointment, tenure, and promotion of faculty who are dually oriented toward teaching and research. The allocation of faculty salary increases should also exhibit a balance between instruction and scholarship.

Colleges and universities inclined toward the Null perspective might also formulate institutional policy that favors a division of effort among faculty. Such a division of effort may be palatable to significant institutional constituents, given the lack of empirical support for the Conflict perspective. Moreover, Bess's (1982) notion of matching faculty professional preferences with organizational needs resonates well with such a division of effort. In the current climate, research universities need to be effective in both teaching and research. Such a need might be efficaciously met by allowing faculty to engage in their most preferred professional activity: teaching or research. One possible negative consequence of such a policy is that higher institutional status is likely to accrue to faculty preferring research. However, this possible negative consequence could be obviated to some extent by applying the policy only to tenured faculty.

In conclusion, public misperceptions about teaching and research have profound significance for colleges and universities. The conclusions and implications offered here might put aside these misperceptions and lead to campus policies that reflect the preferred relationship between teaching and research.

Notes

1. Feldman (1987) reviewed more than twenty-nine studies. However, he used twenty-nine studies for calculation of the average r. These studies contained data that could be used in the meta-analysis.

2. A statistically reliable correlation of +.09 or -.09 was delineated as supporting the Null perspective, since a correlation of this magnitude or lower explains less than 1 percent of the variability between teaching and research.

3. Voeks' study was included in the current analysis because it could be assigned to the Null perspective, given that the association between research and teaching was not statistically significant. Feldman (1987) was unable to include this study in his calculations because needed information was not provided.

4. Although a more recent edition of the Carnegie Classification of Institutions (1994) is available, the 1987 edition was used because of its proximity in time to the reviews conducted by Feldman (1987) and Faia (1976).

References

Aleamoni, L. M., and Yimer, M. "An Investigation of the Relationship between Colleague Rating, Student Rating, Research Productivity, and Academic Rank in Rating Instructional Effectiveness." *Journal of Educational Psychology,* 1973, *64,* 274–277.

Bausell, R. B., and Magoon, J. "The Validation of Student Ratings of Instruction: An Institutional Research Model." Newark, Del.: College of Education, University of Delaware, 1972.

Bayer, A. E. *College and University Faculty: A Statistical Description.* Washington, D.C.: American Council on Education, *Research Reports,* 1970.

Bess, J. L. *University Organization: A Matrix Analysis of the Academic Profession.* New York: Human Science Press, 1982.

Boyer, E. *Scholarship Reconsidered: Priorities of the Professoriate.* Princeton, N.J.: Princeton University Press, 1990.

Braunstein, D. N., and Benston, G.J. "Student and Department Chairman Views of the Performance of University Professors." *Journal of Applied Psychology,* 1973, *58,* 244–249.

Braxton, J. M. "Teaching as a Performance of Scholarly-Based Course Activities." *Review of Higher Education,* 1983, *18,* 379–389.

Bresler, J. B. "Teaching Effectiveness and Government Awards." *Science,* 1968, *160,* 164–167.

Cage, M. C. "States Questioning How Much Time Professors Spend Working with Undergraduate Students," *Chronicle of Higher Education,* August 7, 1991, *37,* p. A1.

Carnegie Foundation for the Advancement of Teaching. *A Classification of Institutions of Higher Education.* Princeton, N.J.: Carnegie Foundation for the Advancement of Teaching, 1987.

Carnegie Foundation for the Advancement of Teaching. *A Classification of Institutions of Higher Education, 1994 Edition.* Princeton, N.J.: Carnegie Foundation for the Advancement of Teaching, 1994.

Centra, J. A. "Research Productivity and Teaching Effectiveness." *Research in Higher Education,* 1983, *18,* 379–389.

Clark, B. R. *Academic Life: Small Worlds, Different Worlds.* Princeton, N.J.: Carnegie Foundation for the Advancement of Teaching, 1987.

Clark, M. J. "Organizational Stress and Professional Performance among Faculty Members at a Small College." Unpublished doctoral dissertation, University of Michigan, 1973.

Dent, P. L., and Lewis, D. J. "The Relationship between Teaching Effectiveness and Measures of Research Quality." *Educational Research Quarterly,* 1976, *1,* 3–16.

Faia, M. A. "Teaching and Research: Rapport or Mesalliance." *Research in Higher Education,* 1976, *4,* 235–246.

Feldman, K. A. "Research Productivity and Scholarly Accomplishment of College Teachers as Related to Their Instructional Effectiveness: A Review and Exploration." *Research in Higher Education,* 1987, *26,* 227–298.

Finkelstein, M. J. *The American Academic Profession: A Synthesis of Social Scientific Inquiry Since World War II.* Columbus, Ohio: Ohio State University Press, 1984.

Fox, M. F. "Research, Teaching, and Publication Productivity: Mutuality Versus Competition in Academia." *Sociology of Education,* 1992, *65,* 293–305.

Freedman, R. D., Stumpf, S. A., and Aguanno, J. C. "Validity of the Course-Faculty Instrument (CFI): Intrinsic and Extrinsic Variables." *Educational and Psychological Measurement,* 1979, *39,* 153–159.

Frey, P. W. "A Two-Dimensional Analysis of Student Ratings of Instruction." *Research in Higher Education,* 1978, *9,* 69–91.

Friedrich, R. J., and Michalak, S. J., Jr. "Why Doesn't Research Improve Teaching? Some Answers from a Small Liberal Arts College." *Journal of Higher Education,* 1983, *54,* 145–163.

Harry, J., and Goldner, N. "The Null Relationship Between Teaching and Research." *Sociology of Education,* 1972, *45,* 47–60.

Hedges, L., and Olkin, L. "Vote-Counting Methods in Research Synthesis." *Psychological Bulletin,* 1980, *88,* 359–369.

Hicks, R. A. "The Relationship between Publishing and Teaching Effectiveness." *California Journal of Educational Research,* 1974, *25,* 140–146.

Hoffman, R. A. "Correlates of Faculty Performance." *College Student Journal,* 1984, *18,* 164–168.

Hoyt, D. P., and Spangler, R. K. "Faculty Research Involvement and Instructional Outcomes." *Research in Higher Education,* 1976, *4,* 113–122.

Kerr, C. *The Uses of the University.* New York: Harper & Row, 1963.

Light, R., and Smith, P. "Accumulating Evidence: Procedures for Resolving Contradictions Among Different Research Studies." *Harvard Educational Review,* 1971, *41,* 429–471.

Linsky, A. S., and Straus, M. A. "Student Evaluations, Research Productivity, and Eminence of College Faculty," *Journal of Higher Education,* 1975, *46,* 89–102.

Marquardt, R. A., McGann, A. F., and Jakubauskas, E. B. "Academic Clients, Scholarly Contributions, Faculty Compensation and Performance Criteria or Shouldn't We Take One More Look Before We Leap . . . ?" *AACSB Bulletin,* 1975, *12,* 13–17.

Marsh, H. W., and Overall, J. W. "Validity of Students' Evaluations of Teaching: A Comparison of Instructor Self Evaluations by Teaching Assistants, Undergraduate Faculty and Graduate Faculty." Paper read at the Annual Meeting of the American Educational Research Association. (ERIC Document Reproduction Service No. ED 177 205), 1979.

McCullagh, R. D., and Roy, M. R. "The Contribution of Noninstructional Activities to College Classroom Teacher Effectiveness." *Journal of Experimental Education,* 1975, *44,* 61–70.

McDaniel, E. D., and Feldhusen, J. F. "Relationship between Faculty Ratings and Indexes of Service and Scholarship." *Proceedings of the 78th Annual Convention of the American Psychological Association,* 1970, *5,* 619–620.

Massy, W. F., and Zemsky, R. "Faculty Discretionary Time: Departments and the 'Academic Ratchet.'" *Journal of Higher Education,* 1994, *65,* 1–22.

Platt, G. M., Parsons, T., and Kirshstein, R. "Faculty Teaching Goals, 1968–1973." *Social Problems,* 1976, *24,* 298–307.

Parsons, T., and Platt, G. "Considerations of the American Academic System." *Minerva,* 1968, *6,* 497–523.

Parsons, T., and Platt, G. *The American University.* Cambridge, Mass.: Harvard University Press, 1973.

Platt, J. R. "Strong Inference." *Science,* 1964, *146,* 347–53.

Rushton, J. P., Murray, H. G., and Paunonen, S. V. "Personality, Research Creativity, and Teaching Effectiveness in University Professors." *Scientometrics,* 1983, *5,* 93–116.

Shils, E. *The Academic Ethic.* Chicago: University of Chicago Press, 1983.

Siegfried, J. J., and White, K. J. "Teaching and Publishing as Determinants of Academic Salaries." *Journal of Economic Education,* 1973, *4,* 90–99.

Stallings, W. M., and Singhal, S. "Some Observations on the Relationships between Research Productivity and Student Evaluations of Courses and Teaching." *American Sociologists,* 1970, *5,* 141–143.

Stavridis, P. G. "Relationships between Student Ratings of Teaching Effectiveness and Certain Criteria Used in Promotion of College Faculty." Unpublished doctoral dissertation, Arizona State University, 1972.

Usher, R. H. "The Relationship of Perceptions of Self, Others, and the Helping Task to Certain Measures of College Faculty Effectiveness." Unpublished doctoral dissertation, University of Florida, 1966.

Veysey, L. R. *The Emergence of the American University.* Chicago: University of Chicago Press, 1965.

Voeks, V. W. "Publication and Teaching Effectiveness." *Journal of Higher Education,* 1962, *33,* 212–218.

Volkwein, F. J., and Carbone, D. A. "The Impact of Departmental Research and Teaching Climates on Undergraduate Growth and Satisfaction." *Journal of Higher Education,* 1994, *65,* 147–167.

Wood, N. J., and DeLorme, C. D., Jr. "An Investigation of the Relationship Among Teaching Evaluations." *Journal of Economic Education,* 1976, *7,* 77–80.

Wood, P. H. "Student and Peer Ratings of College Teaching and Peer Ratings of Research and Service: Four Years of Departmental Evaluation." Paper read at the Annual Meeting of the American Educational Research Association, 1978.

JOHN M. BRAXTON is associate professor of education in the Department of Educational Leadership, Peabody College, Vanderbilt University. His research focuses on the sociology of the academic profession, with an emphasis on faculty role performance and the professional self-regulation of research and teaching.

Critics charge that teaching and research represent incompatible rather than complementary value structures. In this chapter, the relationship between scholarly work and teaching norms held by faculty is examined.

Teaching Norms and Publication Productivity

Anna V. Shaw Sullivan

Teaching, research, and service have historically been the three aspects of academic professionals' work. In recent years, however, some observers and policy makers have criticized academe for being too research oriented, with resulting detrimental effects on college and university students. These critics charge that research and publishing take precedence over teaching, particularly in research institutions (Boyer, 1987, 1990; Study Group, 1984). Such criticisms conclude that teaching and research represent incompatible value structures, create role conflicts in how faculty members divide their professional time and efforts, and result in faculty members shortchanging students by placing their own interests above those of their students.

As the critics' negative view becomes popular, however, we must explore the underlying social processes in order to better determine the relationship between the two roles. One such social process is the normative structure that guides faculty members' behavior.

Informal mechanisms of social control, or normative structures, provide important guides for highly autonomous groups, such as faculty members (Braxton, Bayer, and Finkelstein, 1992; Merton, 1968). These mechanisms, or norms, evolve from the value-driven rules of conduct that define professional groups (Merton, 1968). Further, as members of a professional group, faculty members undergo socialization processes unique to their chosen profession. That is, they acquire not only knowledge and skills in a specific body of knowledge but also attitudes, values, and norms that govern how they perform their roles in the groups they belong to (Merton, Reader, and Kendall, 1957). Moore (1969, p. 869) has suggested that "internalization of norms . . . reduces the necessity of surveillance . . ." which, in turn, allows varying

NEW DIRECTIONS FOR INSTITUTIONAL RESEARCH, no. 90, Summer 1996 © Jossey-Bass Publishers degrees of autonomy for individuals in occupations with professional status. Thus, we would expect faculty members to internalize normative guides for each component of the profession: teaching, research, and service. We would also expect faculty members, as professional representatives, to demonstrate behaviors that exhibit and encourage concern for the welfare of their clients—students—as their first priority.

Little discussion exists, however, of linkages between the norms that support teaching performance and research and publishing productivity. Therefore, in this chapter, I will seek to answer the question: Do faculty who publish a great deal differ in their espousal of four undergraduate teaching norms from those who publish little or nothing? The answer to this question will help shed light on whether faculty members' research activities, indeed, prove detrimental to teaching and to student learning.

Theoretical Framework

In comprehensive and doctoral institutions, the primary mission includes both teaching and research; faculty work includes both instruction and scholarship. Specific disciplines establish and enforce norms (Blau, 1973), with differing levels of commitment to teaching and research serving as normative guides (Biglan, 1973). Braxton and Hargens (1996) suggest that scholarly consensus affects the amount of emphasis that faculty members in specific disciplines place on teaching and research. Low-consensus fields exhibit greater complementarity between teaching and research than do high-consensus fields. In addition, employment in specific institutional and departmental settings reinforces or dissuades an individual's commitment to teaching (Reiss, 1951). The formal peer processes of tenure and promotion reward faculty members. Thus, normative structures that guide professional behavior may arise from a combination of personal and social controls within the academic profession.

In the current educational climate, some scholars suggest that such normative control structures lead faculty members to focus growing amounts of time and energy on pursuits outside of teaching. In order to succeed, faculty members must devote more time to research, at the expense of time dedicated to teaching and related activities. Blackburn and Lawrence (1995) call teaching a "local phenomenon" that carries a far lesser impact on a person's academic career than does research and warn that a career in today's academic environment "depends upon becoming known for one's work" (p. 115) via a high publication rate. Other scholars have suggested that the duties associated with teaching and research require significantly different skills, abilities, and personalities (Finkelstein, 1984; Linsky and Straus, 1975). All of these characteristics—personal, departmental, and institutional—converge to shape academic professionals' perceptions about the value of teaching and research.

Given that social processes guide faculty members' professional behavior, we might expect differences in their espousal of teaching norms among faculty members who publish a great deal and those who publish little or nothing, especially in institutions where greater emphasis is placed on research in order to achieve professional and institutional rewards. Publication productivity provides an index of the value placed on research by the individual academic. Consequently, faculty members who are prolific scholars are less likely to value activities connected to teaching, since these activities detract from the individuals' perceived main professional purpose. Thus, faculty members who place a high value on research are unlikely to be highly committed to teaching. This results in faculty members ascribing less value to norms related to teaching role performance.

In this chapter, I examine the relationship between teaching norms and publication productivity among faculty members in Research I universities, utilizing Braxton, Bayer and Finkelstein's (1992) normative structure for lower-division, undergraduate teaching. The structure, composed of four proscriptive norms including interpersonal disregard, particularistic grading, moral turpitude, and inadequate planning, suggests definitions of appropriate and inappropriate behavior for teaching role performance. Braxton, Bayer, and Finkelstein (1992) define the four norms as follows:

1. The norm *interpersonal disregard* proscribes disregard for the feelings and opinions of students and colleagues.
2. The norm *particularistic grading* eschews failure to use meritocratic criteria in the grading and assessment of student performance.
3. The norm *moral turpitude* prohibits behaviors such as teaching while intoxicated or sexual harassment.
4. The norm *inadequate planning* proscribes behaviors such as failing to provide a class syllabus, not ordering textbooks in time for class, or lack of attention to other details associated with course planning and performance.

Various levels of indignation and outrage may be evoked by violation of teaching norms. Such reactions indicate the social significance of a norm (Durkheim, 1934). Accordingly, the degree of impropriety accorded a given norm will vary as a function of the value an individual places upon teaching role performance.

Methods and Results

This research examines the relationship between teaching norms and publication productivity by using a sample of 114 faculty in the academic disciplines of history, psychology, mathematics, and biology holding full-time appointments in Research I universities. All were doctoral degree-holders, and all held either tenure-track or tenured positions at the rank of assistant professor or higher. The disciplines reflect those used by Braxton, Bayer, and Finkelstein (1992). Biology and mathematics represent high-consensus fields, while psychology and history represent low-consensus fields (Braxton and Hargens, 1996). For the analysis, high-consensus fields were coded as 1 and low-consensus fields as 0.

This research combines two measures of publication productivity: (1) number of journal articles published in the last three years and (2) number of books published in the last three years. These measures were used to form a productivity scale.

In the analysis, multiple regression was used to test the hypothesis that faculty members with higher publication productivity would indicate less value for the teaching norms outlined by Braxton, Bayer, and Finkelstein (1992). Separate regression equations are constructed for each of the four teaching norms and tested at the .05 level of significance. In solving each equation, faculty conformity to each norm is regressed on publication productivity and high- and low-consensus fields.

Overall, the amount of variance explained by the dependent variable on each of the norms is quite small. The norms Interpersonal Disregard (r^2 = .0134), Particularistic Grading (r^2 = .0132), and Moral Turpitude (r^2 = .0135) each account for slightly more than 1 percent of the variance, while the norm Inadequate Planning (r^2 = .0402) accounts for approximately 4 percent of the variance. However, since these equations are statistically nonsignificant, the variability is due to chance. Taking into consideration the small sample size, however, this is not surprising. Further studies with larger, more extensive samples could help to determine whether these results remain consistent.

Results indicate that neither publication productivity (b = .0620, p > .05) nor disciplinary consensus (b = -.1036, p > .05) appears to have an influence on faculty conformity to the norm Interpersonal Disregard. Faculty members also appear consistent in their subscription to the norm Particularistic Grading, regardless of publication productivity (b = .1143, p > .05) or disciplinary consensus (b = .0042, p > .05). On the norm Moral Turpitude, publication productivity (b = .1154, p > .05) and disciplinary consensus (b = -.0264, p > .05) exert no effect on faculty members' ascription of similar value to client welfare. Faculty members also seem to agree on appropriate and inappropriate behaviors and values described under the norm Inadequate Planning, without influence by publication productivity (b = .0611, p > .05) or by disciplinary consensus (b = .1853, p > .05). It therefore appears that faculty members who are prolific scholars do not ascribe less value to the teaching norms as discussed by Braxton, Bayer, and Finkelstein (1992). Thus, they respond similarly to values and behaviors that serve their clients—students.

Conclusions and Implications for Practice

I entered this research expecting that higher publication productivity would be associated with less support for teaching norms generally, given the socialization and reward structures discussed earlier in this chapter. Instead, I found no significant differences. It appears that the mechanisms of social control for teaching are *not* attenuated by high levels of publication productivity. Apparently, faculty members recognize and acknowledge norms that support teaching, while simultaneously participating in the research activities expected in today's academic environment.

In addition, faculty members appear to attach similar value to the welfare of their students, regardless of publication rate. Since this is the case, the continuing discussion of the teaching and research functions should move toward a less dichotomized and more holistic view of their relationship. What, then, may be the implications for policy and practice?

First, these findings suggest that faculty members of varying scholarly productivity subscribe to similar normative structures for teaching role performance. This implies that a universal value system guides the profession and that faculty members are aware of proscribed behaviors. Such a value system serves to push faculty members toward actions that serve the best interests of students rather than the self-interests of faculty members. Thus, it is false for students, parents, administrators, and legislators to assume that scholarly productivity in and of itself represents a detriment to student learning and well-being.

However, faculty members can alleviate some of the negative assumptions about their work. While this study does not address whether or how faculty members enact valued behaviors in the classroom or in their day-to-day contacts with students, we know that student learning and development depend upon more than the simple acknowledgment of appropriate behaviors—they require faculty to carry through on those acknowledgments. Faculty members must demonstrate valued actions and link their research to classroom curricula. When faculty members violate accepted norms, colleagues and institutional leaders at the departmental and college or university level must swiftly intercede on behalf of students' welfare.

Second, institutional leaders must support and encourage faculty members who do demonstrate enactment of these teaching norms. Among other, institution-specific methods, this might occur through college or university awards or other recognitions, as well as through the tenure and evaluation systems within institutions. Such recognition could also provide opportunities for recognition of numerous faculty members in a variety of disciplines.

Finally, members of the profession as a whole must exert greater effort toward communication with the lay public regarding linkages between teaching and research. For legislators, policy makers, parents, and students, such information may be useful in forming balanced opinions and policies about the roles of teaching and research in colleges and universities. It also discourages members of the public from assuming that conflict necessarily exists between teaching and research, instruction and scholarship.

Summary Thoughts

Discussions and concerns about the relationship between teaching and research are likely to continue, both in academic institutions and more broadly in the legislative and public arenas. While a negative tone often drives such discussions, this research provides a more positive view. That is, faculty members, even those who are productive scholars, subscribe to normative structures that support regard for student opinions, meritocratic assessment of student performance, attention to the details of classroom performance, and moral classroom decorum. These faculty attitudes appear to differ only in small and insignificant ways across disciplines.

By exhibiting appropriate and eschewing inappropriate behaviors, faculty members act as guardians of the welfare of their clients—students. Students, then, receive the benefits of both research and teaching activities performed by faculty members. Altering the increasingly popular negative perceptions about the relationship between teaching and research remains a challenge. As additional research provides more details about how normative structures shape faculty work and behavior, we may also learn how to create a better balance between the perceptions and the reality of teaching and research.

References

Biglan, A. "Relationships Between Subject Matter Area Characteristics and Output of University Departments." *Journal of Applied Psychology,* 1973, *57,* 204–213.

Blackburn, R. T., and Lawrence, J. H. *Faculty at Work: Motivation, Expectation, Satisfaction.* Baltimore: Johns Hopkins University Press, 1995.

Blau, P. M. *The Organization of Academic Work.* New York: Wiley, 1973.

Boyer, E. L. *College: The Undergraduate Experience in America.* New York: Harper & Row, 1987.

Boyer, E. L. *Scholarship Reconsidered: Priorities of the Professoriate.* Princeton, N.J.: Carnegie Foundation for the Advancement of Teaching, 1990.

Braxton, J. M., Bayer, A. E., and Finkelstein, M. J. "Teaching Performance Norms in Academia." *Research in Higher Education,* 1992, *33* (5), 533–568.

Braxton, J. M., and Hargens, L. L. "Variation Among Academic Disciplines: Analytical Frameworks and Research, Vol. XI." In J. C. Smart (ed.), *Higher Education: Handbook of Theory and Research.* New York: Agathon Press, 1996.

Durkheim, E. *The Elementary Forms of Religious Life.* London: Allen & Unwin, 1934. (Originally published 1912.)

Finkelstein, M. J. *The American Academic Profession: A Synthesis of Social Scientific Inquiry Since World War II.* Columbus, Ohio: Ohio State University Press, 1984.

Goode, W. J. "Community Within a Community." *Sociological Review,* 1957, *22,* 194–200.

Goode, W. J. "The Theoretical Limits of Professionalization." In A. Etzioni (ed.), *The Semi-Professions and Their Organization.* New York: The Free Press, 1969.

Linsky, A. S., and Straus, M. A. "Student Evaluations, Research Productivity, and Eminence of College Faculty." *Journal of Higher Education,* 1975, *46,* 89–102.

Merton, R. K. *Social Theory and Social Structure.* New York: Free Press, 1968.

Merton, R. K., Reader, G. G., and Kendall, P. L. *The Student Physician: Introductory Studies in the Sociology of Medicine.* Cambridge: Harvard University Press, 1957.

Moore, W. E. "Occupational Socialization." In D. Goslin (ed.), *Handbook of Occupational Socialization.* Chicago: Rand McNally, 1969.

Reiss, A. "Delinquency as a Failure of Personal and Social Controls." *American Sociological Review,* 1951, *16,* 196–207.

Study Group of the Conditions of Excellence in American Higher Education. *Involvement in Learning: Realizing the Potential of American Higher Education.* Washington, D.C.: U.S. Department of Education, 1984.

Zuckerman, H. E. "Deviant Behavior and Social Control in Science." In E. Sagarin (ed.), *Deviance and Social Change*. Beverly Hills, Calif.: Sage, 1977.

ANNA V. SHAW SULLIVAN is a doctoral candidate at Vanderbilt University. Prior to beginning her doctoral work, she served for eight years in higher education administration and teaching.

The level of faculty research activity is widely believed to have a detrimental effect on faculty attitudes toward the improvement of undergraduate education. The authors report findings to the contrary.

Research Activity and the Support of Undergraduate Education

Nathaniel J. Bray, John M. Braxton, John C. Smart

Improving undergraduate education is a major concern of higher education stakeholders: students, parents, faculty members, administrators, state legislators, and members of national associations. A spate of literature has emerged around this concern, some of which pertains to the reform of the undergraduate curriculum. Other literature addresses the betterment of individual teaching and learning.

Because both the curriculum (Toombs and Tierney, 1991) and teaching are instruments of faculty professional practice, curricular reform and improvements in teaching and learning depend on the preferences and expertise of faculty. Such preferences may be shaped by the extent of faculty engagement in research and scholarship.

Some authors claim that research activity creates a faculty culture that is unsupportive of curricular reform. Gaff (1988) asserts that the general education of nonmajors is least important to faculty in this culture of research and scholarship; further, research is also more highly valued than teaching; graduate teaching is more highly regarded than undergraduate teaching; and within undergraduate teaching, advanced courses are preferred over introductory courses.

Research activity also leads to specialization. Massy and Zemsky (1994) contend that such specialization has affected the structure and coherence of the undergraduate curriculum. In particular, the Association of American Colleges report *Integrity in the College Curriculum* (1985) points to a lack of breadth in the general education course requirements of some institutions. Consequently, faculty who are actively engaged in research may be less likely to place importance on acquiring a breadth of knowledge as an important goal of undergraduate education. At base, any efforts to enhance undergraduate education requirements depend on the level of faculty support for this goal.

Faculty research activity may also hinder efforts to improve teaching and learning. Chickering and Gamson (1987) identify seven principles of good practice in undergraduate education from their review of research. Research activity may adversely affect the enactment of one of these seven principles: encouragement of faculty-student contact.

Some authors believe that research and teaching conflict and that undergraduate education consequently suffers (Kerr, 1963; Veysey, 1965; Clark, 1987). Boyer (1990), in *Scholarship Reconsidered: Priorities of the Professoriate,* provides a rationale for this belief, arguing that research activity contends with teaching obligations for time and content. Under this view, teaching loads are reduced, and teaching assistants are assigned to large undergraduate courses (Boyer, 1990). Subsequently, faculty become inaccessible to students as they use their time to pursue scholarly interests. Consequently, faculty who are active researchers may be less accessible to students. As a result, efforts to improve teaching and learning through the encouragement of faculty-student contact, both in and outside of class, may be hampered.

Two hypotheses emerge from the above formulations.

HYPOTHESIS 1: *The greater the level of faculty publication productivity, the lower the importance attached to breadth of knowledge as a goal of undergraduate education.*

HYPOTHESIS 2: *The greater the level of faculty publication productivity, the greater the attitude of faculty inaccessibility to students.*

Little or no research has tested either of these hypotheses. A review of the literature reveals that, while there is a wide array of literature on research productivity and teaching effectiveness, there is substantially less on faculty goals for undergraduate instruction. Indeed, we found no studies directly comparing faculty teaching goals and perceptions of student attributes with research productivity.

However, we found a few studies that examine faculty teaching goals as they relate to discipline differences (Liebert and Bayer, 1975; Platt, Parsons, and Kirshtein, 1976; Platt, Parsons, and Kirshtein, 1978; Smart, 1982; Stark and Morstain, 1978; Quinlan, 1994). Other researchers have examined the relationship between institutional type and faculty teaching goals (Wilson and others, 1975; Guthrie, 1992). Even fewer articles pertain to faculty perceptions of students. Wilson and others (1975) and Fulton and Trow (1974) are among the few studies even mentioning faculty perceptions of students.

Research Procedures

In this chapter, we will be examining a topic that does not receive much exposure in the literature. Our approach was as follows.

Obtaining the Data. We obtained the data for this study from the national survey of faculty conducted by the 1989 Carnegie Foundation for the Advancement of Teaching. The Carnegie study used a two-stage stratified random sample design. In the first stage, a total of 306 institutions were selected for inclusion in the study. These institutions were equally divided among the nine Carnegie Commission classifications, with approximately thirty-four institutions per classification. In the second stage, a random sample was obtained of approximately thirty-two faculty members at each of the 306 institutions that received the questionnaires. A total of 9,996 surveys were distributed, of which 5,450 (54.5 percent) were completed and returned.

The final sample for this study consisted of the 2,106 faculty in research and doctoral-granting universities who provided responses to the Carnegie survey items described below. Our final sample was restricted to those respondents because of our focus on the research productivity of faculty members and its relationship to other measures.

Defining the Variables. Our study investigates the relationships between faculty *research productivity* and the importance faculty attach to the *undergraduate education goal of importance of knowledge breadth* and their attitudes concerning *faculty accessibility to students*. We constructed three levels of *research productivity* from faculty responses to three items: (1) "Approximately how many *articles* have you *ever published* in academic or professional journals?"; (2) "Approximately how many *articles* have you *ever published* in edited collections or volumes?" and (3) "Approximately how many *books or monographs* have you *ever published or edited* alone or in collaboration?" The mean response for these items was computed, and frequency distributions were obtained separately for faculty members in "hard" and "soft" disciplines (Biglan, 1973). The names assigned to each category and range of the mean number of publications per category for faculty in "hard" and "soft" disciplines are:

	"Soft" Fields	*"Hard" Fields*
Low Productivity	0.00 to 2.33	0.00 to 4.33
Moderate Productivity	2.34 to 7.33	4.34 to 13.00
High Productivity	7.34 to 118.33	13.01 to 134.00

Importance of knowledge breadth. Faculty support for the undergraduate acquisition of a breadth of knowledge was researched from a composite of three items reflecting the importance faculty place on three undergraduate education goals: (1) "Provide an appreciation of literature and the arts," (2) "Provide a basic understanding of mathematics and science," and (3) "Provide knowledge of history and the social sciences."[1] This variable was measured by a 5-point Likert scale, ranging from Very Important (1) to Very Unimportant (4), with 5 being No Opinion.

Faculty attitudes about student accessibility. This measure is a composite scale of three items, using responses on a 5-point Likert scale.[2] Those with high scores on this scale agreed that undergraduates "should seek out faculty only during posted office hours" and that undergraduates "expect too much attention." They disagreed with the statement that they "enjoy interacting informally with undergraduates outside the classroom." A high score therefore represents a faculty attitude of being inaccessible to students.

Conducting the Analyses. A 3 x 2 analysis of variance (ANOVA) was used to analyze the data. The two independent variables are Research Productivity (three levels) and Academic Discipline Affiliation (hard and soft); the dependent variables are Faculty Attitudes About Importance of Knowledge Breadth and Accessibility to Students. The $p < .01$ confidence interval is used to interpret the results, in light of the large sample size.

Results

Although there are significant group attitude differences ($p < .01$) among the three research productivity levels on faculty accessibility to undergraduate students, Hypothesis 2 is not supported, as indicated by the factor-based scores for each group (-0.04). Faculty with low research productivity (0.09) tend to espouse an attitude of inaccessibility to undergraduate students more than their colleagues with moderate and high productivity levels (-0.09). The more productive faculty appear to espouse greater accessibility to students.

Discussion and Implications

Possible reforms of the undergraduate curriculum range from altering general education distribution requirements to developing interdisciplinary core courses (Gaff and Wasescha, 1991). The preferences of faculty primarily determine the type and extent of such change. Moreover, changes in general education requirements such as broadening the array of academic subject areas represented in distribution requirements and the development of interdisciplinary core courses largely depend on faculty commitment to acquisition of breadth of knowledge as a goal of undergraduate education.

We hypothesized that faculty who publish at a high rate are less likely to attach importance to this goal than their counterparts who publish at a low rate. However, our findings do not support this hypothesis. Rather, faculty who publish a great deal are as likely as faculty who publish little or nothing to espouse the importance of the acquisition of a breadth of knowledge as a curricular goal.

In research-oriented universities, faculty who are prolific scholars are likely to have high standing among their colleagues. If such scholars voice opposition to alterations in general education requirements requiring a commitment to breadth of knowledge, then other faculty might also be inclined to resist such curricular change. However, the findings of this study suggest that prolific scholars are as likely as their moderate- and low-publishing colleagues to place a high value on this fundamental goal. Hence, we infer that research activity does not shape goal commitments that are likely to attenuate efforts to alter the general education requirements of the undergraduate curriculum.

Improvements in teaching and learning also depend on faculty inclinations. Attitudes fostering faculty availability to undergraduate students is one such inclination. The successful implementation of one of Chickering and Gamson's (1987) seven principles of good practice in undergraduate education depends on faculty willingness to be accessible to students. We anticipated that faculty who are prolific publishers are less likely to espouse such a willingness. Our findings indicate the contrary: prolific scholars appear to be more favorably disposed toward contact with students than their low-publishing colleagues. Thus, research activity appears to pose no barrier to the enactment of Chickering and Gamson's (1987) principle that faculty and student contact should be encouraged. In contrast, research inactivity more likely presents such a hurdle.

Implications for Research

Scholars have debated the congruence between attitudes and behaviors. Some scholars such as Rokeach (1973) contend that attitudes and values shape behavior. In contrast, social psychologists such as Ajzen and Fishbein (1977) contend that strong relationships between behavior and attitudes occur when the correspondence between an espoused attitude and its antecedent behavior is high.

Given such divergent viewpoints, institutional researchers and scholars of the improvement of undergraduate education should study the relationship between espoused commitments to breadth of knowledge acquisition as a curricular goal and behavior pertinent to curricular deliberations and implementation. Such scholars should also focus on faculty attitudes toward accessibility to students and behavioral indicators of this attitude. The influence of research and scholarly activity on both of these relationships should also be examined further. Such research would not only expand our understanding of the relationship between teaching and research but would also inform the efforts of individual colleges and universities to improve undergraduate education. Finally, further research should be done to explore whether research activity influences these attitudes or if these attitudes are the result of other qualities that also produce active researchers.

Implications for Administrators

The findings of this study run contrary to public perceptions about research activity and its influence on curricular change and the enhancement of teaching and learning. College and university administrators should use these findings to shape public debate on research activity and teaching. Administrators interested in the improvement of undergraduate education need not be wary of an unreceptive predisposition of prolific scholars toward such efforts.

Instead, college and university administrators might enlist the support of such faculty in both curricular change and the development of policies and programs designed to encourage faculty-student contact. The prestige and institutional standing enjoyed by prolific scholars might motivate other faculty members to participate in efforts to change the curriculum and encourage faculty-student interactions. An awareness of these formulations should inform and improve the practice of public policy makers, college and university administrators, and scholars.

Notes

1. This scale was obtained from a factor analysis of survey items assessing the degree of importance of seven goals for undergraduate education. Three factors were delineated: Knowledge Acquisition, Knowledge Integration, and Knowledge Application. This study uses knowledge acquisition because it is pertinent to Hypothesis 1.

2. This scale was derived from a factor analysis of survey items pertaining to faculty perceptions of students. Two factors were identified: student unpreparedness and faculty inaccessibility. Faculty inaccessibility is used herein because of its direct relevance to Hypothesis 2.

References

Ajzen, I., and Fishbein, M. "Attitude-Behavior Relations: A Theoretical Analysis and Review of Empirical Research." *Psychological Bulletin,* 1977, *84,* 888–918.

Association of American Colleges. *Integrity in the College Curriculum: A Report to the Academic Community.* Washington, D.C.: Association of American Colleges, 1985.

Biglan, A. "Relationship between Subject Matter Area Characteristics and Output of University Departments." *Journal of Applied Psychology,* 1973, *57,* 204–213.

Boyer, E. *Scholarship Reconsidered: Priorities of the Professoriate.* Princeton, N.J.: The Carnegie Foundation for the Advancement of Teaching, 1990.

Chickering, A. W., and Gamson, Z. E. "Seven Principles for Good Practice in Undergraduate Education." *AAHE Bulletin,* 1987, *39,* 3–7.

Clark, B. R. *Academic Life: Small Worlds, Different Worlds.* Princeton, N.J.: Carnegie Foundation for the Advancement of Teaching, 1987.

Fulton, O., and Trow, M. "Research Activity in American Higher Education." *Sociology of Education,* 1974, *47,* 29–73.

Gaff, J. G. *General Education Today: A Critical Analysis of Controversies, Practices and Reforms.* San Francisco: Jossey-Bass, 1988.

Gaff, J. G., and Wasescha, A. "Assessing the Reform of General Education." *The Journal of General Education,* 1991, *40,* 51–68.

Guthrie, D. S. "Faculty Goals and Methods of Instruction: Approaches to Classroom Assessment." In J. L. Ratcliffe (ed.), *Assessment and Curricular Reform.* New Directions for Higher Education, no. 80, San Francisco: Jossey-Bass, 1992.

Kerr, C. *The Uses of the University.* New York: Harper & Row, 1963.

Liebert, R. J., and Bayer, A. E. "Goals in Teaching Undergraduates: Professional Reproduction and Client-Centeredness." *The American Sociologist,* 1975, *10,* 195–205.

Massy, W. F., and Zemsky, R. "Faculty Discretionary Time: Departments and the 'Academic Ratchet.'" *Journal of Higher Education,* 1994, *65,* 1–22.

Platt, G. M., Parsons, T., and Kirshtein, R. "Faculty Teaching Goals, 1968–1973." *Social Problems,* 1976, *24,* 298–307.

Platt, G. M., Parsons, T., and Kirshtein, R. "Undergraduate Teaching Environments: Normative Orientations to Teaching Among Faculty in the Higher Education System." *Sociological Inquiry,* 1978, *43,* 3–21.

Quinlan, K. M. "Uncovering Discipline-Specific Interpretations of the 'Scholarship of Teaching': Peer Review and Faculty Perceptions of Scholarly Teaching." Paper presented at the Annual meeting of the Association for the Study of Higher Education, 1994.

Rokeach, M. *The Nature of Human Values.* New York: The Free Press, 1973.

Smart, J. C. "Faculty Teaching Goals: A Test of Holland's Theory." *Journal of Educational Psychology,* 1982, *74* (2), 180–188.

Stark, J. S., and Morstain, B. R. "Educational Orientations of Faculty in Liberal Arts Colleges: An Analysis of Disciplinary Differences." *Journal of Higher Education,* 1978, *49,* (5), 420–437.

Toombs, W., and Tierney, W. G. *Meeting the Mandate: Renewing the College and Departmental Curriculum.* ASHE-ERIC Report No. 6. Washington, D.C.: George Washington University, Association for the Study of Higher Education, 1991.

Veysey, L. R. *The Emergence of the American University.* Chicago: University of Chicago Press, 1965.

Wilson, R. C., Gaff, J. G., Dienot, E. R., Wood, L., and Barry, J. L. *College Professors and Their Impact on Students.* New York: Wiley, 1975.

NATHANIEL J. BRAY is a doctoral candidate in higher education at Vanderbilt University.

JOHN M. BRAXTON is associate professor in the Department of Educational Leadership at Peabody College of Vanderbilt University.

JOHN C. SMART is professor in the Department of Leadership at the University of Memphis in Memphis, Tennessee.

*Evidence about the compatibility of the teaching and research roles
remains inconclusive. In this chapter, the authors present data
collected at a Research I institution on the relationship between
research productivity and specific instructional practices and
faculty-student contact. The findings represent a stringent test
of the Complementarity hypothesis.*

The Research Versus Teaching Debate: Untangling the Relationships

Deborah Olsen, Ada Simmons

In the 1970s and 1980s, numerous studies were carried out to determine whether the two central roles in an academic career—teaching and research—complement each other or conflict. Much of this literature was summarized in an article by Feldman in 1987. Despite the obvious significance of the issue to faculty workload policy and reward systems, the evidence remains inconclusive. The most promising scenario indicated a positive but small relationship between research productivity and teaching; a less sanguine analysis suggested that the two roles are independent. After Feldman's extensive review and its disappointing conclusions, research on the issue diminished.

While difficulties in establishing empirical parameters of the research-teaching relationship may have given researchers pause, public concern over the rising costs of higher education and the erosion of undergraduate education has fueled rhetoric and debate over the impact of research activity and its supporting reward system on instruction (Fairweather, 1993; "Thoughts from the First Forum on Faculty Roles and Rewards," 1993; Winston, 1994). Thus, our ability to provide accurate and meaningful information about the integrity of faculty roles, or the lack of it, has particular importance at this time.

Role conflict theories suggest that proportionately less time and energy will be invested in one role as more is invested in another (Goode 1960; Merton 1957). Under this scenario, faculty should devote less time and energy to teaching in an environment that rewards and values research productivity. Recent work within higher education indicates just this: the faculty reward system and the current assignment of salary and prestige constrains and undermines faculty investment in teaching (Diamond and Adam, 1993; Fairweather, 1993; Fairweather and Rhodes, 1995; Moore and Amey, 1993). This "conflict" viewpoint maintains that even if the quality of instruction is fairly high, more time and energy invested in teaching (and less on research) would improve the quality of undergraduate education still further (Massy and Wilger, 1995). More specifically, it has been argued that faculty highly invested in their research agenda will be less interested in an undergraduate curriculum that is broader, simpler, and less intellectually challenging than the subject matter of their research. In turn, these faculty may be less attuned to students' level of understanding and their learning needs (for example, Faia, 1976; Friedrich and Michalak, 1983, cited in Feldman, 1987). Moreover, research scholarship often requires time and solitude, and faculty who are oriented toward research are likely to find they have neither the time to be as available to students nor the personal inclination to cultivate the interpersonal skills that best facilitate faculty-student interaction (Fairweather, 1993; Feldman, 1987).

Theories endorsing *complementarity* of roles (see Chapter One) such as the theories of Sieber (1974) and Thoits (1987) suggest that there are synergies between roles that can be exploited through personal commitment and interest. The higher education literature also provides evidence that teaching and research roles are mutually supportive. Centra (1983) suggests that faculty active in research are more likely to keep their courses fresh with the recent developments in their fields, to hold higher expectations of their students, to communicate both the involvement and enthusiasm they feel for their disciplinary subject to students, as well as an important sense that knowledge grows over time. Further, the organizational and cognitive skills underlying the ability to successfully frame, analyze, and present complex research questions are skills that should transfer well to instruction. From a broad list of "instructional dimensions," Feldman (1987) found four to be most strongly associated with research productivity: (1) knowledge of the subject matter, (2) intellectual expansiveness, (3) preparation and organization of the course, and (4) clarity of course objectives and requirements. Feldman's review and meta-analysis of over forty studies also indicated, however, that not all aspects of teaching and research are as closely allied. In particular, research productivity and student rapport were statistically independent. Thus, while the conflict hypothesis that research faculty would be less available and less attuned to students was not confirmed, neither was a positive relationship confirmed.

More recently, Volkwein and Carbone (1994) revisited the relationship between teaching and research from a different and very interesting vantage point, examining more macro-level effects of department culture and reward system (that is, as oriented toward teaching or research) on undergraduates' academic growth and integration. Volkwein and Carbone found the most positive academic outcomes for students occurred in departments that valued both teaching and research, arguing that research productivity can benefit the instructional climate. Importantly, these researchers also found that the impact of departmental culture on undergraduates' academic experience was quite small when compared with the impact of actual classroom experiences and faculty-student contact. These findings lend support to Feldman's (1987) ear-

lier contention that actual pedagogical practices and classroom-related disposi-
tions mediate between research productivity and overall teaching effectiveness.

The study presented here addresses the widely held view that research
exercises a negative impact on the quality of teaching. The implication is that
highly productive researchers "economize" on the time and energy they allocate to teaching by constraining teaching tasks and reducing time-consuming
involvement with students. By logical extension, we can apply this theoretical
perspective to more specific teaching practices and hypothesize that if a conflict model is correct, higher levels of research productivity should encourage
the use of teaching formats, modes of evaluation, and pedagogical techniques
that are geared more toward personal efficiency than instructional effectiveness. For example, this view suggests that highly productive researchers would
teach fewer introductory level courses, rely more heavily on a predictable,
teacher-centered lecture format and concomitantly use fewer "active learning"
techniques, maintain lower expectations of students, and more frequently use
objective tests to evaluate students rather than more open-ended measures that
require more time to grade. The present study includes specific measures of
instructional practices to explore what areas of instruction may be enhanced
or inhibited by a strong research profile.

Unfortunately, current findings with regard to the relationship between
research productivity and instruction, even those that imply a positive relationship, are often vague about the activities and dimensions that link the two
roles (negatively or positively). Feldman's review (1987) suggests that research
productivity enhances certain pedagogical skills of faculty (for example, their
knowledge, organization, intellectual expansiveness, and clarity) but that rapport with students was independent of (or even negatively related to) performance in research. There is significant literature to indicate the importance of
faculty-student contact to student retention and to the overall quality of students' academic experiences (Endo and Harpel, 1982; Terenzini and Wright,
1987; Terenzini, Springer, Pascarella, and Nora, 1995), as well as to faculty's
own satisfaction with teaching (Olsen and Simmons, 1995). Thus, a lack of
faculty-student rapport would be well worth addressing, even among faculty
who are talented researchers. We will thus also examine the effects of research
productivity on the quality and quantity of interactions that faculty have with
undergraduate students.

The present study offers some advantages over prior research on the relationship between academic roles. First, research productivity is measured over
a multiyear time frame using institutional data actually used in salary-setting
and other decision-making processes. Second, this study taps data recounting
actual practices that faculty use in the classroom and in dealing more generally with students. This is in contrast to most previous work, which has
assessed teaching effectiveness through summative student evaluations. Finally,
critics often claim that at large research institutions, research activity is overem-
phasized, producing a faculty characterized by fine research and scholarship
skills but lacking in teaching effectiveness and interest. The present study, set

in a large, Research I institution, provides a context in which such claims can be examined using empirical data.

Methods

One hundred fourteen faculty in the College of Arts and Sciences and the School of Business at a large, public Research I institution were interviewed. A stratified random sample of participants was selected from a pool of faculty who had taught at least one undergraduate course in the previous two-year period. Approximately 70 percent were tenured, 80 percent were male, and 90 percent were white (males and whites were slightly overrepresented in the sample). Faculty from the College of Arts and Sciences constituted about 90 percent of the sample, with 40 percent in the humanities, 30 percent in the social sciences, and 30 percent in the hard sciences, proportions that closely approximate the actual distribution of faculty in these disciplinary areas.

The semistructured interview format enabled exploration of a wide range of teaching-related issues such as teaching load, instructional goals, methods of evaluation of student learning, attitudes toward students and teaching, and the proportion of time faculty allocate to teaching, research, and service. In addition, participants completed the Wingspread "Seven Principles for Good Practice in Undergraduate Education" inventory (Chickering, Gamson, and Barsi, 1989), which consists of seven subscales: faculty-student contact, student cooperation, active learning techniques, prompt student feedback, respect for diverse styles of learning, high expectations of performance, and time on task (all subscales $a \geq .70$). Wingspread items were coded on a 1- to 5-point scale, with 1 indicating most frequent use of a practice. Low subscale scores thus indicate high frequency of use of a set of pedagogical techniques. Faculty were also administered a questionnaire on teaching stress ($a = .75$) (modified from Gmelch, Lovrich, and Wilke, 1984) and were asked an interview question about how satisfied they were with their own teaching.

For ninety-two of the original sample, teaching data were supplemented with information related to research productivity, drawn from summary reports of activities submitted annually by faculty to their departments and the campus. Activity report data were collected for three years (the year of the interview as well as the two years preceding it). Measures of research productivity included number of books, refereed articles, edited books, book chapters, book reviews, books translated, technical reports, invited talks, conference papers, and dissertations chaired. Weights were assigned to the various research productivity measures in a manner that reflected departmental criteria and convention. More specifically, a weight of 3 was assigned to published books, 2 to edited books and refereed articles, 1 to book chapters, book reviews, translations, technical reports, and invited talks, and .5 to dissertations chaired and conference presentations. An annual average of research productivity was computed.

Using the frequency distributions of annual research productivity, three levels of research productivity were established (low, medium, and high) within humanities, social sciences, and hard sciences. Levels of research productivity were then collapsed across disciplines, so that low producers ($n = 31$), regardless of discipline, now made up one group, medium producers ($n = 32$) another, and high producers ($n = 29$) a third.

Results

On average, faculty spend about 44 percent of their time on teaching and 34 percent of their time on research. These figures are close to those reported nationally by faculty at Research I institutions (43 percent for teaching and 29 percent for research, National Center for Educational Statistics, 1990). Moreover, our data indicate a significant negative relationship between the amount of time spent on research and teaching ($r = -.58$, $p < .01$) and between the amount of time spent on teaching and a strong professional interest in research ($r = -.50$, $p < .01$). When levels of research productivity were considered, analysis of variance revealed that the percentage of time devoted to teaching ($F = 2.72$, $p < .07$) differed among the three groups, with the high-productivity group spending the least ($\bar{x} = 38.2$ percent) and the low-productivity group spending the most ($\bar{x} = 46.3$ percent) time on teaching, but differences did not reach the $p < .05$ level. The effect of productivity level was more pronounced for percentage of time devoted to research ($F = 4.14$, $p < .05$), whereas the low-productivity group ($\bar{x} = 28.6$ percent) and high-productivity group ($\bar{x} = 40.2$ percent) differed significantly.

Analysis of variance was used to investigate the effect of level of research productivity on specific aspects of undergraduate teaching using the three levels of research productivity as the independent variable. Post hoc tests (Scheffe, $p < .05$) were then used to identify group means that differed significantly from others. Contrary to a conflict model, faculty with a high level of research productivity were no less likely to teach at the 100 level ($F = .99$, $p > .05$) or 200 level ($F = 1.08$, $p > .05$), no more likely to use a lecture format ($F = .58$, $p > .05$), no less likely to use a discussion format ($F = .97$, $p > .05$), no less likely to supplement a textbook with primary sources ($F = 1.34$, $p > .05$) or make use of out-of-class resources ($F = 3.16$, $p > .05$) than other faculty with lower levels of research productivity. Nor did methods of evaluating students differentiate faculty groups. All faculty tended to rely heavily on in-class tests and to assign projects, papers and homework less frequently and to weight them less heavily in determining course grades. Low-productivity faculty reported requiring significantly more out-of-class study hours from students than other faculty groups. However, the general pattern of low-productivity faculty emphasizing time on task to a greater degree than other faculty groups was not confirmed by the Wingspread subscale.

A cluster of behaviors taken from the interview instrument and the Wingspread Good Practices subscales on "student contact" and "prompt student feedback" were examined to see whether highly productive researchers limited their contact with undergraduate students, a finding that would add fuel to critics' claims that research-minded faculty have less rapport with students. Highly productive researchers were no more or less likely to contact their students who demonstrated academic difficulty (a low-incidence behavior) than other groups, nor did their scores on the Wingspread faculty-student contact subscale evidence less frequent interaction. High-level researchers did display a few characteristics suggesting some tendency to limit involvement with students, however. For example, although highly productive research faculty maintained as many office hours as less productive, proportionally fewer students, especially those in lower-level courses, came to their office hours. Moreover, the high-productivity group provided students with significantly less short-term feedback about their learning and performance (Wingspread subscale). This type of feedback tends to be more informal and continuous and requires more day-to-day communication between faculty and student. It is not surprising, then, that the high-productivity group also reported knowing their students less well than did faculty in the other two groups.

Discussion and Recommendations

By and large, findings failed to support the current view that many positive teaching behaviors are inversely related to research productivity. Faculty with strong research profiles did not avoid teaching lower-level undergraduate classes, did not rely more on lecture and less on active learning techniques, and did not use more multiple-choice tests in their classes than other faculty. On the other hand, the contention that more productive researchers demonstrate higher levels of pedagogical skills was not confirmed either. It could be argued that the absence of significant differences in methods of student evaluation, use of active learning techniques, and use of nontext, nonclassroom resources indicated potential areas for instructional development, irrespective of research productivity level. Faculty with a high level of research productivity did appear to have somewhat less contact with students, although the Wingspread subscale for this dimension failed to demonstrate significant differences among the three groups.

In sum, findings suggest that research and teaching performance are unrelated when teaching is defined by instructional practices, and they are negatively related when particular aspects of faculty-student contact are considered. There is little evidence that the two roles are complementary. The fact that a majority of faculty reported being more interested in teaching than research suggests that the ability to "expand" time and energy to satisfy multiple role demands may be more constrained than Sieber (1974) thought, even when the commitment is high.

Dramatic changes in today's students—their backgrounds, learning styles, and expectations—along with concomitant developments in pedagogy designed to address contemporary students' needs, may necessitate greater change in the delivery of undergraduate education than has been undertaken to date. Accountability issues and the criticism that higher education neglects undergraduate teaching may, in fact, be due more to a mismatch between faculty and students' expectations of faculty and collegiate instruction than unwillingness on faculty members' part to spend time or effort on teaching. The issue is not that faculty have failed in their teaching of undergraduates but that a new set of pedagogical goals and skills may be required. In particular, we need to ask whether we have been as vigilant in promoting and rewarding exploration, currency, and creativity in instruction as we have in research.

Some concrete recommendations can be made based on the present work. First, both faculty and students benefit significantly from faculty-student contact, and yet this may be an area negatively affected by research demands. Institutions can offer instructional development programs that provide faculty with strategies for staying in better contact with their students—methods that are not simply one-on-one meetings. For example, faculty could be introduced to classroom assessment techniques (Angelo and Cross, 1993) that allow faculty to monitor their students' mastery of course materials using short-term, ungraded assignments. Use of such techniques deepens faculty members' and students' understanding of student learning and needs and, evidence suggests, makes the faculty-student relationship closer and more informed. Technology can also help faculty stay in better touch with students. Faculty are increasingly using e-mail (listservs, electronic classrooms) to communicate with students.

Second, universities and colleges should encourage more widespread use of active learning techniques that appear especially well suited to the learning styles of contemporary students. More recent cohorts of freshmen come to college with experience in collaborative learning, a foundation faculty can build on as they become more familiar with the value of this technique and the variety of ways it can be implemented. Debates, role plays, and simulations also help make learning more "hands on" for students. Approaches to student writing have been rethought and revamped to emphasize writing as a tool for thinking and learning, while reducing the amount of grading required; assigning microthemes is one example (Bean, Drenk, and Lee, 1982).

Third, we need to broaden teaching evaluation processes, relying less exclusively on student evaluations and becoming more tolerant of the "failures" that are inevitable when pioneering new instructional methods and techniques. Institutions must affirm faculty's current teaching efforts, while providing support and incentives to improve and use more of the "best practices" identified by Wingspread and others. Moreover, institutions must promote instructional innovation at every level in tenure and promotion decisions as well as annual reviews.

Fourth, institutions should provide undergraduates with opportunities to learn first-hand from faculty about their research. Such programs not only provide a direct and visible link between the two roles that are the mainstay of academic life but offer students important insight into the research mission of a university and how the boundaries of knowledge are expanded through research. If institutions wish to see faculty invest more in instruction and yet maintain research productivity, they must actively help faculty find mechanisms and strategies for better coordination of these two demanding roles. The current study suggests that individual accommodation alone will not be sufficient to create a fundamental change in the instructional context but that organizations must vigorously encourage and support faculty's efforts to teach better and to more successfully integrate teaching and research efforts.

References

Angelo, T. A., and Cross, K. P. *Classroom Assessment Techniques: A Handbook for College Teachers.* San Francisco: Jossey-Bass, 1993.

Bean, J. C., Drenk, D., and Lee, F. D. "Microtheme Strategies for Developing Cognitive Skills." In C. W. Griffin (ed.), *Teaching Writing in All Disciplines.* New Directions for Teaching and Learning, no. 12. San Francisco: Jossey-Bass, 1982.

Centra, J. A. "Research Productivity and Teaching Effectiveness." *Research in Higher Education,* 1983, *18,* 379–389.

Chickering, A. W., Gamson, Z. F., and Barsi, L. M. "Seven Principles for Good Practice in Undergraduate Education: Faculty Inventory." Milwaukee: Johnson Foundation, 1989.

Diamond, R. M., and Adam, B. E. (eds.). *Recognizing Faculty Work: Reward Systems for the Year 2000.* New Directions for Higher Education, no. 81. San Francisco: Jossey-Bass, 1993.

Endo, J. J., and Harpel, R. L. "The Effect of Student-Faculty Interaction on Students' Educational Outcomes." *Research in Higher Education,* 1982, *16,* 115–138.

Faia, M. A. "Teaching and Research: Rapport or Mesailliance." *Research in Higher Education,* 1976, 235–246.

Fairweather, J. S. "Faculty Rewards Reconsidered: The Nature of Tradeoffs." *Change,* July/August 1993, *25,* 44–47.

Fairweather, J. S., and Rhodes, R. A. "Teaching and the Faculty Role: Enhancing the Commitment to Instruction in American Colleges and Universities." *Educational Evaluation and Policy Analysis,* 1995, *17,* 179–194.

Feldman, K. A. "Research Productivity and Scholarly Accomplishment of College Teachers as Related to Their Instructional Effectiveness: A Review and Exploration." *Research in Higher Education,* 1987, *26,* 227–298.

Gmelch, W. H., Lovrich, N. P., and Wilke, P. K. "Sources of Stress in Academe: A National Perspective." *Research in Higher Education,* 1984, *20,* 477–90.

Goode, W. J. "A Theory of Role Strain." *American Sociological Review,* 1960, *25,* 483–496.

Massy, W. F., and Wilger, A. K. "Improving Productivity: What Faculty Think About It and Its Effect on Quality." *Change,* July/August 1995, *27,* 10–20.

Merton, R. K. *Social Theory and Social Structure.* Glencoe, Ill.: The Free Press, 1957.

Moore, K. M., and Amey, M. F. *Making Sense of the Dollars: The Costs and Uses of Faculty Compensation.* ASHE-ERIC Higher Education Report No. 5. Washington, D.C.: American Association for the Study of Higher Education, 1993.

National Center for Education Statistics. *Faculty in Higher Education Institutions, 1988.* Washington, D.C.: U.S. Department of Education, 1990.

Olsen, D., and Simmons, A. "Enhancing Satisfaction with Teaching: Restructuring Rewards." Paper presented at the Association for Institutional Research, Boston, May 1995.

Sieber, S. D. "Toward a Theory of Role Accumulation." *American Sociological Review,* 1974, *39,* 567–578.

Terenzini, P., and Wright, T. "Influences on Students' Academic Growth during Four Years of College." *Research in Higher Education,* 1987, *26,* 161–179.

Terenzini, P. T., Springer, L., Pascarella, E. T., and Nora, A. "Academic and Out-of-Class Influences on Students' Intellectual Orientations." *Review of Higher Education,* 1995, *19,* 23–44.

Thoits, P. A. "Negotiating Roles." In F. J. Crosby (ed.), *Spouse, Parent, Worker: On Gender and Multiple Roles.* New Haven, Conn.: Yale University Press, 1987.

"Thoughts from the First Forum on Faculty Roles and Rewards." *Change,* July/August 1993, *25,* 18–19.

Volkwein, J. F., and Carbone, D. A. "The Impact of Departmental Research and Teaching Climates on Undergraduate Growth and Satisfaction." *Journal of Higher Education,* 1994, *65,* 147–167.

Winston, G. C. "The Decline in Undergraduate Teaching: Moral Failure or Market Pressure?" *Change,* September/October 1994, *26,* 8–15.

DEBORAH OLSEN is assistant dean in the Office of Academic Affairs at Indiana University, Bloomington, Indiana.

ADA SIMMONS is a doctoral candidate in higher education administration at Indiana University, Bloomington, Indiana.

The relationship between faculty publication productivity and the cognitive complexity of student examination questions is examined. Results show that scholars who publish books and those who publish fewer articles ask more critical-thinking questions. Publishing more articles seems to negatively influence the asking of such questions.

Faculty Productivity and the Complexity of Student Exam Questions

Robert M. Johnson, Jr.

Growing pressure for reform in higher education is bringing many long-standing assumptions in the academy under public scrutiny. Among the most controversial of these beliefs is the notion that good researchers make the best teachers. Critics assert that these scholarly roles conflict with each other. They contend that the emphasis placed on scholarly publishing, which underlies the prestige of Research I and II universities, is a detriment to teaching. On the other hand, the rationale behind the belief that good researchers make the best teachers is that research and teaching are, in fact, complementary scholarly roles. Presumably, the good researcher knows his or her field well, is enthusiastic, and communicates both knowledge and enthusiasm in the classroom. Neither proponents nor critics of this line of reasoning, however, have marshaled much evidence either to support or contradict it (Terenzini and Pascarella, 1994).

Part of the problem is in determining how the quality of research and of teaching skills can be measured. How can anyone know whether a research emphasis actually supports or detracts from the quality of teaching? I will address that question here. Critical thinking is important to both teaching and research.

The scholarly skills of critical thinking, particularly analysis and synthesis, are essential to crafting research and scholarship (Toombs, 1975; Braxton and Toombs, 1982; Braxton and Nordvall, 1988). Constructing coherent lines of reasoning in the process of designing research requires making inquiries that integrate related areas of knowledge; poor questions rarely prompt fruitful avenues of investigation and typically lead to poor research. Likewise, critical thinking skills are critical to the teaching role. As Carpenter, Doig, and Doig

(1988) note, "Recent national reports and publications identify critical think-ing as an essential ingredient of higher education" (p. 33). Thus, these skills are highly valued in the role of the teacher as well as the researcher.

The role of the teacher is multidimensional, demanding a range of schol-arly activities (Braxton, 1983; Braxton and Nordvall, 1988). Consequently, the exercise of critical thinking skills in "out-of-class conversations with stu-dents, assigned written course activities, course and comprehensive exami-nations, and the conceptualization of thesis or dissertation topics" (Braxton and Nordvall 1988, p. 147) is to be expected. Previous research suggests that the construction of examination questions, which requires critical thinking skills, may be one dimension of the college teaching role that is clearly affected by the research role (Braxton, 1983; Braxton, 1993; Braxton and Nordvall, 1985, 1988).

Test construction is a vital aspect of the teaching role, both for assessment and instruction (Lord, 1970; Jacobs and Chase, 1992). A well-designed test should support and reinforce other aspects of the instructional process. In fact, "the effectiveness of testing is enhanced by careful attention to the principles of test construction and to the use to be made of the results" (Gronlund, 1988, p. 1). Test items are accordingly the "most specific and concrete level of expres-sion of [instructional] objectives" (Krathwohl and Payne, 1971, p. 41). The percentage of questions requiring critical thinking skills is thus illustrative or indicative of other aspects of a scholar's performance of the teaching role.

If the roles of researcher and teacher are complementary, the teacher who is also an active researcher should be more likely to ask a greater percentage of questions requiring critical thinking skills than teachers who are less active as researchers. The purpose of this study is to see whether or not that is true. Are university faculty who publish frequently more likely to ask course exam-ination questions that require critical thinking than are faculty who publish rarely or even moderately?

Bloom's Taxonomy

Bloom's (1956) taxonomy is a useful tool for distinguishing between different cognitive tasks and the skills necessary to accomplish them. The taxonomy dif-ferentiates between six hierarchically arranged categories or levels of cognitive complexity: knowledge, comprehension, application, analysis, synthesis, and evaluation. In coding the examination items, analysis, synthesis, and evalua-tion categories were collapsed into the single category, "higher order think-ing"—"critical thinking" in this study—recognizing research by Krathwohl and Payne (1970) and Madus, Woods, and Nuttal (1973), who have "challenged the rank and operational independence of these three categories" (Braxton 1993, p. 663).[1] Examination items that require higher order thinking should reflect the demand for a greater level of course content understanding than an item requiring simply recall, or knowledge, in the taxonomy.

Studies by Braxton (1993) and Braxton and Nordvall (1985) establish the utility of these taxonomic distinctions in rating course examination items with respect to academic rigor. In this study, I have extended the direction of that research to examine the relationship between the research productivity of the teacher and the rigor demanded in the examination. Consistent with the assumption of role complementarity, teachers who are active researchers would be expected to ask critical thinking questions more frequently than teachers who are not active researchers.[2]

Research Design

To control for the possible effects of differences between disciplines and examination construction, I selected a random sample of 560 faculty members holding full-time appointments at Research I and II universities in the academic disciplines of biology, chemistry, history, and psychology. I selected faculty from these four disciplines based on Creswell and Roskens' (1981) research on Biglan's typology of academic disciplines.

Creswell and Roskens' research suggests that "disciplines differ on such dimensions as the goals of academic departments, scholarly or research productivity, and preferences and time commitments for research and teaching" (Braxton 1993, p. 664). Consequently, the percentage of certain types of examination questions might vary simply for reasons related to the expectations and norms of the academic discipline. Similarly, with respect to publication frequency and type, disciplines of high paradigmatic development (Kuhn, 1970; Lodahl and Gordon, 1972) such as chemistry or biology may be more likely to emphasize or value the production of articles over books; accordingly, the publication of articles was separated from the publication of books in the survey, and I divided the disciplines into two groups, high and low consensus. High-consensus disciplines are biology and chemistry. The low-consensus disciplines are history and psychology.

Two measures of publication productivity were used: (1) the number of journal articles and (2) the number of books published during the previous three years. The number of articles were divided into three levels of publication productivity: (1) the publication of two or fewer items during that time span constituted a low publication rate; (2) three to five articles constituted moderate productivity; (3) of six or more articles constituted high productivity. The number of books published was divided into two levels of publication productivity: (1) no books published and (2) one or more books published over the three-year time span.

A two-stage cluster sampling design was used in the study. In the first stage, forty research universities were randomly selected (Braxton, 1993). From their catalogues, a random sample of faculty members in each of the four academic disciplines was derived for a total of 560 faculty members. The faculty members received a cover letter with instructions to send a representative sample of their undergraduate course examinations and a survey instrument requesting information about the faculty member and the course correspond-ing to the examination. From the 560 faculty members, I obtained 115 use-able examinations; however, 202 of the recipients did not meet sampling criteria and were subtracted from the sample for an adjusted sample size of 358 and a 32.1 percent response rate.

Two measures of examination item content were used: (1) the percentage of knowledge questions asked and (2) the percentage of critical thinking ques-tions asked. When parts of an examination item plumbed different levels of cognitive complexity, the question was divided into subquestions. Trained coders classified each question or subquestion into one of these two categories. The proportion of each type of question to the total questions or subquestions yielded the percentage of each type of examination item.

Analysis of Results

A two-way analysis of variance was used to determine whether the percentage of knowledge questions or critical thinking questions varied with publication productivity or academic discipline.

Rate of Article Publication. With academic discipline controlled, the percentage of knowledge questions asked on the examinations varies with the publication productivity of articles ($F = 2.3$, $p < 0.10$). Post-hoc mean com-parisons indicate that scholars publishing three to five articles over a three-year period asked more knowledge questions than those with two articles or fewer over the same time span (39.5 percent versus 29.7 percent). Those scholars publishing six or more articles over three years asked knowledge questions at an even higher rate (45.5 percent) than those publishing three to five articles (39.5 percent).

With academic discipline held constant, the percentage of critical think-ing questions asked also varies with the rate of productivity of article publica-tion ($F = 6.3$, $p < .01$). Post-hoc mean comparisons reveal that those teachers who published a little (two articles or fewer) or even moderately (three to five articles) differed significantly from those who published six or more articles, in that those who published at a high rate asked fewer critical thinking ques-tions than the other two groups. The group with the highest rate of produc-tivity asked only 6.6 percent critical thinking questions on their examinations, whereas the groups with low publication rates asked 22.7 percent, and the group with moderate productivity asked 21.1 percent critical thinking ques-tions.

Rate of Book Publication. Holding academic discipline constant, I found that the percentage of knowledge questions asked did not vary significantly with the publication productivity of books ($F = 1.6$, $p = .10$), but the percent-age of higher order thinking questions did vary according to book productiv-ity ($F = 17.3$, $p = .01$). Post-hoc mean comparisons suggest that those who published one book or more during the three-year period asked a greater percentage of critical thinking questions than those who published no books during that period. Those teachers who published even one book asked 36.6 percent higher order thinking questions; those without a book published during that period asked only 12.7 percent.

Implications and Conclusions

Those who publish articles at a comparatively low or moderate rate tend to ask fewer knowledge questions and more critical thinking questions than those scholars who publish at a high rate. The group of scholars who are highly invested in the publication of articles appear to do so at the expense of attention to important aspects of their pedagogical responsibilities. In this case, the focus of intervention should rest on the development of teaching skills among those scholars who are absorbed in the production of research articles.

On the other hand, those who publish books asked more critical thinking questions than those who published no books over the three-year period. Perhaps the sustained focus on a single book topic and its connections to other matters of inquiry is more compatible with sustained attention to teaching skills than the potentially more fragmented approach associated with a high rate of article production.

Teachers who publish books and teachers who publish articles at a low or moderate rate have similar characteristics with respect to examination construction. Possibly, the two groups of researchers overlap; that is, scholars at Research I and II universities who focus more on the publication of books than on the production of articles constitute a large percentage of both groups. More likely, though, is the conclusion that a more balanced approach to the scholarly roles leads to a greater quality of performance in the classroom. Certainly, those who invest themselves deeply in research productivity appear to construct their examinations at a level of cognitive complexity that is significantly lower than that of their colleagues who publish at a low or moderate rate.

The message for academic and faculty development officers might be that re-emphasizing student learning while retaining faculty attention to research means promoting less fragmented, more focused research activities leading to moderate article or book production. However, the differences in the types of research required to produce books and articles are often structured within disciplines and are therefore beyond the influence of university academic officers.

Promoting collaborative research might permit faculty to maintain a balanced emphasis on article publication productivity while retaining the necessary focus on cognitive complexity in the classroom. As disciplines do exert a strong influence on the accepted forms of research activity (Bayer and Smart, 1988; Fox and Faver, 1984), collaborative research could prove detrimental to tenure attainment in some disciplines, especially low-consensus disciplines, in which collaboration has never garnered the prestige of individual research (Baldwin and Austin, 1995). Collaborative teams, however, usually make significant contributions to research. New and short-term collaborative teams often demonstrate the greatest creativity and innovation, while mature and long-term teams often provide the best context for high productivity (Baldwin and Austin, 1995). A potential direction for future study, then, is to examine the relationship between collaborative research and cognitive complexity in the classroom.

University academic officers face a great challenge in promoting faculty vigilance to the teaching role if the social and financial rewards are dependent upon success or productivity in the research role. Socialization into the scholarly roles begins long before scholars are hired into faculty positions. Striking the balance between research and teaching priorities must begin with the development of scholarly behaviors, norms, and values in the graduate program rather than in the faculty role.

The growing pressure on institutions of higher education to justify their costs is driving legislatures to demand assessment programs to monitor outcomes. As this movement increases in scope, and it seems that it will, attention to student cognitive development and higher order thinking will become critical matters for university academic officers. Analyzing examination questions is perhaps one of the best ways to assess faculty expectations for student learning (Braxton and Nordvall, 1988).

Public scrutiny challenges us to develop different models of the interactions among knowledge production, teaching, and student learning.

Notes

1. Braxton and Nordvall (1988) and Braxton (1993, p. 663) reanalyze these categories as the single category "critical thinking" to be consistent with the notion as Winter, McClelland, and Stewart (1981) present it.

2. The size of a class, however, does not appear to have a statistically significant connection with the percentage of knowledge or critical thinking questions on examinations (Braxton 1993, 666).

References

Baldwin, R. G., and Austin, A. E. "Toward Greater Understanding of Faculty Research Collaboration." *The Review of Higher Education, 19,* 1995, 45–70.

Bayer, A. E., and Smart, J. C. "Author Collaborative Styles in Academic Scholarship." Paper presented at the annual meeting of the American Educational Research Association, New Orleans, April 1988.

Biglan, A. "The Characteristics of Subject Matter in Different Academic Areas." *Journal of Applied Psychology, 57,* 159–203, 1973a.

Biglan, A. "The Relationship between Subject Matter Characteristics and the Structure and Output of University Departments." *Journal of Applied Psychology, 57,* 204–213, 1973b.

Bloom, B. S. (ed.). *Taxonomy of Educational Objectives: Cognitive Domain.* New York: McKay, 1956.

Braxton, J. M. "Teaching as a Performance of Scholarly Based Course Activities: A Perspective on the Relationship Between Teaching and Research." *The Review of Higher Education, 7,* 21–34, 1983.

Braxton, J. M. "Selectivity and Rigor in Research Universities." *Journal of Higher Education, 64,* 657–675, 1993.

Braxton, J. M., and Nordvall, R. C. "Quality of Graduate Department Origin of Faculty and its Relationship to Undergraduate Course Examination Questions." *Research in Higher Education, 28,* 145–159, 1988.

Braxton, J. M., and Nordvall, R. C. "Selective Liberal Arts Colleges: Higher Quality as well as Higher Prestige?" *Journal of Higher Education, 56,* 538–554, 1985.

Braxton, J. M., and Toombs, W. "Faculty Uses of Doctoral Training: Consideration of a Technique for the Differentiation of Scholarly Effort from Research Activity." *Research in Higher Education, 16,* 265–282, 1982.

Carpenter, C., Doig, B., and Doig, J. C. "Assessing Critical Thinking Across the Curriculum." In J. H. McMillan (ed.), *Assessing Students' Learning.* New Directions for Teaching and Learning, no. 34. San Francisco: Jossey-Bass, 1988.

Creswell, J., and Roskens, R. "The Biglan Studies of Differences Among Academic Areas." *Review of Higher Education, 4,* 1–16, 1981.

Feldman, K. "Research Productivity and Scholarly Accomplishment of College Teachers as Related to Their Instructional Effectiveness: A Review and Exploration." *Research in Higher Education, 26,* 227–298, 1987.

Fox, M. F., and Faver, C. A. "Independence and Cooperation in Research: The Motivations and Costs of Collaboration." *Journal of Higher Education, 55,* 347–59, 1984.

Gronlund, N. E. *How to Construct Achievement Tests.* (4th ed.). Englewood Cliffs, N.J.: Prentice Hall, 1988.

Jacobs, L. C., and Chase, C. I. *Developing and Using Tests Effectively: A Guide for Faculty.* San Francisco: Jossey-Bass, 1992.

Krathwohl, D. R., and Payne, D. A. "Defining and Assessing Educational Objectives." In R. L. Thorndike (ed.), *Educational Measurement.* (2nd ed.). Washington, D.C.: American Council on Education, 1971.

Kuhn, T. S. *The Structure of Scientific Revolutions.* (2nd ed.). Chicago: University of Chicago Press, 1970.

Lodahl, J. B., and Gordon, G. "The Structure of Scientific Fields and the Functioning of the University Graduate Departments." *American Sociological Review, 37,* 57–72, 1972.

Lord, F. M. "Some Test Theory for Tailored Testing." In Wayne H. Holtzman (ed.), *Computer-Assisted Instruction, Testing, and Guidance.* New York: Harper & Row, 1970.

Madus, G. F., Woods, E. M., and Nuttal, R. L. "A Causal Model Analysis of Bloom's Taxonomy." *American Educational Research Journal, 10,* 253–262, 1973.

Terenzini, P. T., and Pascarella, E. T. "Living with Myths: Undergraduate Education in America." *Change, 26,* 28–32, 1994.

Toombs, W. "Awareness and Use of Academic Research." *Research in Higher Education, 7,* 701–717, 1975.

Winter, D., McClelland, D., and Stewart, A. *A New Case for the Liberal Arts: Assessing Institutional Goals and Student Development.* San Francisco: Jossey-Bass, 1981.

ROBERT M. JOHNSON, JR., *is director of institutional research at Belmont University, Nashville, Tennessee.*

There is some evidence that research productivity is positively associated with teaching effectiveness, as measured by student achievement. In this chapter, the author examines whether research activity actually enhances certain pedagogical skills and thus increases student learning.

Triangulating the Relationships Among Publication Productivity, Teaching Effectiveness, and Student Achievement

Michael Gavlick

The relationship between research and teaching is complex, involving several dimensions and many variables. The relative importance allocated to the roles of research and teaching is likely to vary across institutional types, academic disciplines, and faculty career stages. These contextual differences, in turn, give rise to differences in faculty attitudes and values regarding both teaching and research, norms that govern their individual and collective behavior, and specific goals they work toward. Sorting through such a puzzle of dimensions and associated variables requires the careful alignment of many pieces.

The purpose of this chapter is to outline a possible link between the research proclivity of college instructors and the academic achievement of their students, a commonly accepted measure of teaching effectiveness. To the extent that the faculty roles of research and teaching are truly complimentary, such a link might exist. While no theory now relates the research proclivity of college instructors to the academic performance of their students, extensive research has related both research activity and student academic performance to certain teaching activities. This research might provide evidence for a link between faculty research activity and student academic achievement through certain teaching behaviors.

To identify such a link, I integrated two extensive analyses of literature. Using meta-analysis, Feldman (1987) established a small but statistically significant correlation between research activity and student perceptions of overall instructional effectiveness. Cohen (1981) also used meta-analytic methods to validate student evaluations as good indicators of instructional effectiveness, as measured by student achievement. In so doing, Cohen used only studies with objective measures of student achievement, such as examination grades. Perhaps there are things done by faculty who publish (studied by Feldman) that promote student achievement (studied by Cohen) that can be identified by mapping across various dimensions of teaching (identified by both Feldman and Cohen). Figure 6.1 depicts such a possible relationship.

Figure 6.1 suggests that research activity shapes or enhances certain teaching behaviors, which, in turn, result in greater student achievement. As a means of establishing such a relationship, we will first look briefly at Feldman's findings and then at those of Cohen.

Research Productivity and Instructional Effectiveness

In 1987, Feldman carefully reviewed existing literature on the connection between research productivity, or scholarly accomplishment, of faculty members and their teaching effectiveness as perceived by students. After isolating twenty-nine studies that pertained, he derived an average correlation of $r = +.12$ ($p < .001$).

In conducting his work, Feldman suspected that some instructional factors might correlate positively with research productivity and others that might correlate negatively, thereby masking true relationships. This same rationale would also apply to global or overall ratings, since students would need to mentally sum or "aggregate" across a variety of specific instructional areas in order to arrive at an overall or general assessment. Feldman, therefore, analyzed studies for specific indicators of pedagogical attitudes and practices and course characteristics, and the relationship of these variables to research productivity. Table 6.1 summarizes those results.

Table 6.1 suggests that four instructional dimensions are most associated with research productivity, with correlations ranging from 0.15 to 0.21. These are teacher's knowledge of subject, intellectual expansiveness, preparation/organization, and clarity of course objectives and requirements. Perhaps a somewhat broader label that would meaningfully distinguish this group of salient dimensions would be *instructor knowledge and preparation*.

Instructional Effectiveness and Student Achievement

Cohen (1981) confirms that student ratings of instructors are valid measures of teaching effectiveness, as measured by student achievement. The average

Figure 6.1. Rudimentary Causal Model of the Impact of Research Activity on Student Achievement

Research Activity ⟶ Teaching ⟶ Student
(Publication Productivity)   Behaviors   Achievement

Table 6.1. Average Correlation Between Research or Scholarly Productivity and Student-Rated Effectiveness of Teacher on Various Instructional Dimensions

Instructional Dimension	Average (Weighted) N	(Weighted) r	Combined (Weighted) Z	p
No.1. Teacher's Stimulation of Interest in the Course and its Subject Matter	6-5/6	+.08	+2.001	.045
No.2. Teacher's Enthusiasm (for Subject or for Teaching)	3-1/2	+.09	+1.518	.129
No.3. Teacher's Knowledge of the Subject	5	+.21	+6.618	<.001
No.4. Teacher's Intellectual Expansiveness (and Intelligence)	2	+.15	+2.330	.020
No.5. Teacher's Preparation; Organization of the Course	5-1/3	+.19	+5.307	<.001
No.6. Clarity and Understandableness	7-1/6	+.11	+3.785	<.001
No.7. Teacher's Elocutionary Skills	—	—	—	—
No.8. Teacher's Sensitivity to, and Concern with, Class Level and Progress	1-1/4	+.07	+1.166	.244
No.9. Clarity of Course Objectives and Requirements	3-1/2	+.18	+3.172	.002
No.10. Nature and Value of the Course Material (Including Its Usefulness and Relevance)	4-1/2	+.06	+2.064	.039
No.11. Nature and Usefulness of Supplementary Materials and Teaching Aids	2	+.08	+2.416	.016
No.12. Perceived Outcome or Impact of Instruction	5-5/6	+.10	+2.524	.011
No.13. Instructor's Fairness; Impartiality of Evaluation of Students; Quality of Examinations	4-5/6	−.001	+0.773	.464
No.14. Personality Characteristics ("Personality") of the Instructor	1	+.12	+1.022	.307
No.15. Nature, Quality, and Frequency of Feedback from Teacher to Students	1-1/2	+.07	+0.849	.396
No.16. Teacher's Encouragement of Questions and Discussion, and Openness to Opinions of Others	3-7/12	−.0005	+0.617	.537
No.17. Intellectual Challenge and Encouragement of Independent Thought (by the Teacher and the Course)	2-7/12	+.09	+3.024	.003
No.18. Teacher's Concern and Respect for Students; Friendliness of the Teacher	4	+.05	+0.326	.744
No.19. Teacher's Availability and Helpfulness	4-7/12	−.0004	+0.915	.360

Note: No studies relating specifically to instructional dimension No. 7 were incorporated in this meta-analysis.

Source: Table 6.1 is taken from Feldman's 1987 study and used with permission.

correlation between an overall instructor rating and student achievement of $r = +.43$ that he obtained via an extensive meta-analysis of existing literature is strong evidence.

In developing his study, Cohen also confronted the problem of the multidimensional structure of most rating instruments. He recognized that not all of the dimensions should relate to objective measures of student achievement to the same extent. Consequently, in addition to overall course and instructor assessments and student self-ratings of their progress, he adopted and assessed seven dimensions of teaching. Table 6.2 summarizes Cohen's findings along these dimensions.

Not surprisingly, the instructor skill dimension is strongly associated with student achievement ($r = +.50$). The skill dimension represents the overriding quality to which students respond when rating instructors. Typical items are: "The instructor has a good command of the subject matter," and "The instructor gives clear explanations." Interestingly, structure is also strongly correlated with student achievement ($r = +.47$). Cohen notes, "Students of instructors who have everything going according to schedule, use class time well, explain course requirements, and in general have the class well organized tend to learn more than students of instructors who are not well organized" (p. 302).

Mapping Through Instructional Effectiveness

Both Cohen and Feldman note that instructional effectiveness needs to be broken down into component dimensions to reveal any masking of counterbalancing effects. Perhaps because the two researchers derived their respective disaggregation of instructional effectiveness at different times and from different literature, they do not immediately appear analogous. They can, however, be compared in view of the results obtained, triangulating the salient dimensions of instructional effectiveness. Cohen found that instructor skill and the

Table 6.2. Average Rating-Achievement Correlations

	N	r
Overall Course	22	.47
Overall Instructor	67	.43
Skill	40	.50
Rapport	28	.31
Structure	27	.47
Difficulty	24	-.02
Interaction	14	.22
Feedback	5	.31
Evaluation	25	.23
Student Progress	14	.47

amount of structure in the course are more important for student learning than are certain interpersonal aspects (instructor rapport, interaction, and feedback). This is consistent with Feldman's findings. The four dimensions Feldman found most strongly related to research productivity (teacher's knowledge of subject [$r = +.21$], intellectual expansiveness [$r = +.15$], preparation/organization [$r = +.19$], and clarity of course objectives/requirements [$r = +.18$]) can be thought of as relating to Cohen's notions of instructor skill and structure. Consequently, faculty who publish (Feldman) might actually promote student achievement (Cohen) by tending to exercise certain knowledge and pedagogical skill more than do faculty who publish little or not at all.

By thus superimposing the work of Feldman (1987) and Cohen (1981), we produce a model linking research activity to student achievement via certain specific teaching behaviors.

Toward a Model of Research Activity, Teaching Behaviors, and Student Achievement

Previous investigators have found it useful and logical to break instructional effectiveness down into different configurations of component teaching behaviors. As noted in this chapter, Feldman (1987) worked with nineteen dimensions[1] and Cohen (1981) used seven. Such work provides us with alternative configurations of specific teaching behaviors that have varying associations with research activity and student achievement. Figure 6.2 is an expansion of Figure 6.1, which illustrates two alternative pathways as potential components in a rudimentary causal model of the impact of research activity on student achievement.

Figure 6.2 illustrates how a possible causal path from research activity to student achievement might be affected by how teaching behavior is specifically conceptualized. This suggests the importance of carefully selecting specific

Figure 6.2. Rudimentary Causal Model of the Impact of Research Activity on Student Achievement, Showing Alternative Configurations of Teaching Behaviors

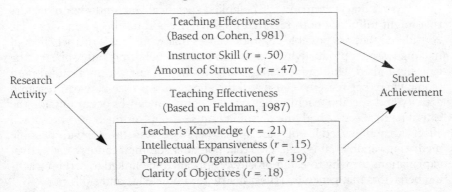

teaching behaviors for use in outlining causal path alternatives for empirical examination.

Feldman (1987) looked specifically at a number of variables taken from the literature as potentially mediating between research activity and teaching behavior. He stated these in terms of propositions. Although Feldman (1987) found only weak evidence of the mediating variables he looked for, propositions incorporating such variables as integral to a theoretical model should be systematically explored. Two possibilities, taken from Feldman (1987), are mentioned here for illustrative purposes.

The first proposition appears to contain four possible mediating variables, which are italicized here for ease of identification. Being productive in research helps teachers not only *keep abreast* in their field and *gain understanding* of the subject matter they teach but also to increase their *intellectual vitality* and *involvement.* Any of these variables ostensibly resulting from research productivity could result in differing specific teaching behaviors with subsequent effects on student achievement. Indeed, the four variables highlighted in this proposition actually approximate the teaching behaviors [Feldman's (1987) instructional dimensions] of the teacher's *knowledge of the subject,* and the teacher's *intellectual expansiveness.* These are analogous to Cohen's notion of instructor skill. Differences among such possible mediating variables (italicized above) can be quite subtle but nonetheless important.

A second proposition more directly reflects teaching behaviors previously identified by Feldman (1987): Research productivity fosters a teacher's own *intellectual self-discipline,* which may manifest itself in *better organization* of the course and of classroom lectures, which relate to Cohen's notion of structure. Furthermore, *clearer explanations* of course material (relating to instructor skill) would also result. In this example, the mediating variable of *intellectual self-discipline* results in the teaching behaviors of the teacher's *preparation/ organization of the course, clarity and understandableness,* and possibly in *clarity of course objectives and requirements.* It therefore seems evident that a rigorous search for variables that might mediate between research and teaching behavior should and would occur in conjunction with the careful delineation of specific teaching behaviors for use in outlining causal path alternatives.

Beyond that, Feldman (1987) looked specifically at a number of factors that might influence both research productivity and teaching behaviors. He considered these as possible common causes that would have the net effect of making research productivity and certain teaching behaviors only appear to be causally linked. Unlike mediating variables that occur within a causal path (somewhere between the cause and the effect, in this case between research activity and specific teaching behaviors), common causes occur outside the causal path, affecting both the presumed cause and its (erroneously) presumed effect. An abbreviated list of these appear below. As was the case with possible mediating variables, it is suggested that potential common causes exist as rival explanations for why research proclivity appears to be linked to certain teaching behaviors that generally reflect instructor knowledge and skill.

- Faculty Academic Rank and Age
- Faculty Time and Effort
- Faculty Personal Attributes and Personality Characteristics (such as, General Ability; Intelligence and Intellectual Curiosity; Responsibleness, Persistence, and Orderliness; Ascendancy, Forcefulness, and Leadership; Supportiveness, Tolerance, and Warmth; and Sociableness and Extraversion).

Contextual or conditional issues transcend any possible mediating factors and common causes, including individual faculty characteristics. That is, predicted relationships might hold in some situations and under certain circumstances but not in others. Examples of contextual variables include instructor experience, academic discipline, institutional type, and the type of learning outcomes targeted. Regarding institutional type, it is possible that research and teaching tend to be inversely related at the extremes, such as at research universities and community colleges. Ruscio (1987) reports that between the extremes of high-quality research universities and community colleges, research activity and institutional quality decrease in tandem. A counterbalancing emphasis on effective teaching just might increase in parallel. If so, comprehensive universities might be a more promising context within which to demonstrate a causal relationship between research proclivity and student learning. Regarding learning outcomes, Pascarella and others (forthcoming) found that faculty organization/preparation facilitated students' general cognitive skills more so than did faculty skill/clarity. Viewing this work as demonstrating a contextual phenomenon, perhaps higher order learning outcomes are facilitated by different teaching behaviors than are outcomes relating to the acquisition of (factual) information. The point is that contextual considerations such as instructor experience, academic discipline, institutional type, and type of learning outcomes should be explored in tandem with possible mediating variables and common causes.

Research Implications

In this chapter, I have hypothesized a rudimentary causal model linking faculty research activity and student achievement (Figure 6.2) based primarily on the work of Cohen (1981) and Feldman (1987). Specific teaching behaviors appear to be the key linking mechanisms. These hypothesized relationships certainly need to be empirically tested. Path analysis is a procedure that could estimate the magnitude of the predicted linkages postulated in such a model. While relying on multiple regression as its principle statistical technique, path analysis would identify and measure possible indirect effects as well as the direct effects depicted by the model's theoretical paths. Such indirect effects occur as a result of unseen, mediating variables and would appear to be particularly important at such an early stage of theoretical development. (For a fuller discussion of this approach, see Wolfle, 1985.)

I have emphasized the importance of distinguishing among and isolating certain specific teaching behaviors that might relate to both faculty scholarship and student learning. In so doing, possible mediating variables and common causes should be explored. Beyond that, certain contextual considerations such as differences among academic disciplines and institutional types should be taken into consideration. While the work suggested herein will be complex, the possibility of empirically demonstrating a link between faculty research activity and student achievement would appear to justify the effort.

Note

1. In a 1989 study, Feldman used twenty-eight instructional dimensions or teaching behaviors. Whether one chooses to describe teaching in terms of a few or many specific behaviors would seem to primarily reflect one's purposes and the nature of the data that are related in terms of those teaching dimensions.

References

Cohen, P. A. "Student Ratings of Instruction and Student Achievement: A Meta-Analysis of Multisection Validity Studies." *Review of Educational Research,* 1981, *51* (3), 281–309.

Feldman, K. A. "Research Productivity and Scholarly Accomplishment of College Teachers as Related to their Instructional Effectiveness: A Review and Exploration." *Research in Higher Education,* 1987, *26* (3), 227–298.

Feldman, K. A. "The Association between Student Ratings of Specific Instructional Dimensions and Student Achievement: Refining and Extending the Synthesis of Data from Multisection Validity Studies." *Research in Higher Education,* 1989, *30* (6), 583–645.

Pascarella, E., Edison, M., Nora, A., Hagedorn, L., and Braxton, J. "Effects of Teacher Organization/Preparation and Teacher Skill/Clarity on General Cognitive Skills in College." *Journal of College Student Development,* 1996, 37(1), 7–19.

Ruscio, K. P. "Many Sectors, Many Professions." In B. R. Clark (ed.), *The Academic Profession.* Los Angeles: University of California Press, 1987.

Wolfle, L. M. "Applications of Causal Models in Higher Education." In J. C. Smart (ed.), *Higher Education: Handbook of Theory and Research,* Vol 1. New York: Agathon Press, 1985.

MICHAEL GAVLICK *is a doctoral candidate in higher education administration, Department of Educational Leadership, Peabody College, Vanderbilt University.*

*The ways in which faculty work, including teaching and research,
occur within a cultural context. The author suggests ways to analyze
departmental and institutional cultures and offers suggestions for
academic leaders interested in nurturing cultures that value both
teaching and research.*

Institutional and Departmental Cultures: The Relationship Between Teaching and Research

Ann E. Austin

The ways in which faculty members balance and relate their teaching and
research is not solely the result of individual preferences. As members of disciplines, departments, and institutions, faculty members do their work in a
cultural context. In the first part of this chapter, I will examine the ways in
which departmental and institutional cultures pertain to the relationships
between teaching and research in higher education. Second, I will suggest
strategies that can be used to explore the nature of departmental and institutional cultural contexts and how they relate to faculty teaching and research
endeavors. Finally, I will consider ways in which academic leaders may influence departmental and institutional cultures so that teaching and research may
both be more fully valued and supported.

Academic Cultures

Culture pertains to how groups of people create meaning and understanding
in their experience. According to Geertz (1973, p. 5), individuals within
groups create "webs of meaning" that include their shared values, assumptions, and interpretations. Kuh and Whitt (1988) refer to culture as "the collective, mutually shaping patterns of norms, values, practices, beliefs, and
assumptions that guide the behavior of individuals and groups. . . ." [Culture,
in brief, is] "an interpretative framework for understanding and appreciating
events and actions" (pp. 12–13). Because these norms, beliefs, values, and
assumptions are deeply embedded and enduring, not just easily made and

changed preferences, cultural change typically occurs slowly, sometimes in response to significant events, problems, or crises (Peterson and Spencer, 1990). Those interested in understanding the culture or "organizational glue" (Peterson and Spencer, 1990, p. 7) binding a group can look for expressions and clues in the members' behavior patterns, in symbols and rituals used by the group, and in the myths and stories shared (Deal and Kennedy, 1982; Peterson and Spencer, 1990; Schein, 1985).

Faculty members live and work within several cultures simultaneously (Austin, 1990; Bergquist, 1992; Clark, 1984; Light, Marsden, and Corl, 1972). Of particular relevance to the ways in which they value, balance, and relate teaching and research are their disciplinary cultures, institutional cultures, and departmental cultures. The disciplinary culture links faculty in similar fields across institutions; the institutional culture links faculty across disciplines within a single institution; and the departmental culture results from the interaction of disciplinary and institutional norms and values at a particular location.

The Cultures of the Disciplines. Disciplines serve as the "primary units of membership and identification within the academic profession" (Clark, 1987, p. 7). Becher (1981) explains, "Disciplines are . . . cultural phenomena: they are embodied in collections of like-minded people, each with their own codes of conduct, sets of values and distinctive tasks" (p. 109).

Various researchers and theorists have explored and categorized the dimensions on which disciplines vary. For example, Lodahl and Gordon (1972) focus on the extent of paradigm development as the central classifying variable. Biglan's work (1973), which is frequently used in higher education studies, classified disciplines in eight categories, based on their positions on three dimensions: hard-soft (whether a single paradigm or theory guides work in the field), pure-applied (whether there is emphasis on application), and life-nonlife (whether living systems are studied). Building on this and other theoretical work, Braxton and Hargens (1996) point out that disciplines generally can be classified on the basis of "the levels of consensus their members exhibit on such matters as appropriate theoretical orientations, proper research methods, and the relative importance of research questions." High-consensus and strong paradigm development tend to characterize the physical sciences. Lower consensus and weaker paradigm development characterize the social sciences; and lowest consensus and paradigm development characterize the humanities.

Disciplines classified across these dimensions differ in their cultures, with the differences expressed in a variety of ways—in the questions asked, the quality criteria used, the patterns of publication, and the ways in which colleagues interact (Austin, 1990, 1992; Becher, 1981, 1984, 1987; Clark, 1984; Kuh and Whitt, 1988). Of particular relevance for this chapter are the variations in disciplinary cultures in the ways teaching and research are related, and in particular, whether teaching and research are complementary or conflicting.

Braxton and Hargens (1996) point out that the degree of scholarly consensus within departments serves as a mediator in the relationship between teaching and research. After reviewing a wide array of studies and comparing high-consensus disciplines with low-consensus disciplines, they concluded that faculty in high-consensus disciplines, where paradigms are clearly defined, demonstrate more orientation to research, higher publication rates, and proportionately more time on research. Department chairpersons in these fields also tend to emphasize research goals more heavily. Apparently, "neither complementarity nor conflict is apparent in hard disciplines" (Braxton, forthcoming).

Calling the soft paradigm fields "affinity disciplines" to reflect their greater orientation to teaching, Braxton (forthcoming) compares the habits of faculty in these fields with those of their high-consensus, hard paradigm colleagues. He reports that faculty in low-consensus disciplines are more oriented to teaching, spend more time on their teaching, and express more interest in it. Furthermore, in the soft fields, faculty tend to emphasize student growth and development and the goals of broad general education more strongly than their colleagues in the hard fields. Additionally, they are more likely to emphasize active learning and the development of students' oral and written skills, as well as to use student-centered teaching activities. Feldman's work (1987) reviewing a range of studies reached similar conclusions about the differences in high-consensus and low-consensus disciplines with regard to the relationship between teaching and research. He concluded that the relationship between teaching and research performance was insignificant in high-consensus disciplines and moderate in low-consensus disciples.

Throughout graduate school, students are socialized to the practices, norms, and values embedded in the culture of their respective disciplines. Then, as their careers as faculty members develop, the disciplinary societies— invisible colleges that link those in similar subfields—and disciplinary publications maintain the strength and power of the discipline's values.

Institutional Cultures. In addition to the disciplinary cultures, institutional cultures significantly affect the relationship between teaching and research. A variety of elements contribute to an institution's culture, including its mission, organizational structure, physical environment, and student and faculty characteristics (Austin, 1990, 1992; Peterson, Cameron, Jones, Mets, and Ettington, 1986). Of particular importance to the teaching-research balance is the institutional mission, which affects how new faculty are socialized, what tasks are expected, how much time is available for teaching or research, and what activities are rewarded (Austin, 1990; Clark, 1963; Kuh and Whitt, 1988; Ruscio, 1987). Where research is a primary institutional mission, faculty tend to spend comparatively more time on research and engage in specialized research activities. Where teaching is a strong institutional mission, faculty often engage in less-specialized research; research efforts often may connect fields and synthesize or reintegrate previously discovered knowledge. Those faculty with heavy teaching responsibilities sometimes find over time that they have increasing difficulty making connections to the increasingly specialized disciplines (Ruscio, 1987).

Though every institution has its own distinct culture, it is possible to generalize about cultural characteristics that are frequently found in particular institutional types (Austin, 1990; Clark, 1985, 1987). In universities, the disciplinary cultures tend to dominate more strongly than in other institutional types. The culture emphasizes the value of research productivity and research specialization, and faculty often interact with colleagues in their respective disciplines by traveling to conferences and engaging in projects that cross institutional boundaries. In a study of institutions that emphasize both teaching and research, Astin and Chang (1995) found that those in their sample of 212 institutions with a high research orientation and low student orientation were all research universities. It is noteworthy that in the past five years, a number of universities have been taking stock of their cultures and seeking ways to more fully address and integrate their multiple missions, which include not only research but teaching and professional service roles. The challenge is considerable to find ways to develop and nurture new cultural values in environments where norms and policies have predominantly emphasized research for a number of decades.

In comprehensive universities, which are often state-supported, the institutional culture often involves conflicting messages, as faculty must carry heavy teaching loads while facing expectations that they model the research university faculty in research productivity. Integration of teaching and research is not the norm so much as are competing expectations. In the community colleges, teaching is the primary institutional mission and value. Full-time faculty members teach numerous courses, and the large cadre of part-timers are connected with the institution solely to perform teaching assignments. Research is not viewed as an institutional mission or value.

The prestigious liberal arts colleges are the most likely institutional type to nurture institutional cultures in which both teaching and research are valued. Astin and Chang (1995) found that the institutions in their sample that emphasized both teaching and research were private, prestigious liberal arts colleges. In these institutions, faculty devote considerable attention to their teaching and to the broad development of their students; additionally, the faculty are supported in their on-going efforts to stay connected with their disciplines and contribute to knowledge development. The institutional culture cherishes the importance of and the relationship between teaching and research. In contrast, the less-selective liberal arts colleges are often places where teaching is the sole expectation and where limited financial resources and heavy demands on faculty time preclude both faculty research activity and travel to maintain connections with colleagues.

Departmental Cultures. As the location where disciplinary and institutional cultures intersect, each department has a unique culture also (Austin, 1994; Becher, 1981, 1984). In addition to the influence of disciplinary and institutional cultural values and norms, a department's culture is affected by the particular leadership style of the chairperson, the personal characteristics of the students and faculty, the physical environment, the department's history within the specific institution, and its relationship to other units within the college or university. Over time, a department develops its own values and norms regarding the relationship between teaching and research, including how and to what extent faculty interact about teaching or research issues, the extent to which there are opportunities for public discussions about teaching or research (for example, seminars, faculty meetings), the resources provided for each of these activities, and the ways in which teaching and research are rewarded. Focusing on the academic department as the unit of analysis, Volkwein and Carbone (1994) examined departmental research and teaching climates, as measured by deans' ratings, student ratings, and various behavioral measures. They conclude that the departments they studied varied considerably in their research and teaching climates.

Because a department is the site of intersection for the discipline and institution, faculty may experience conflicting messages about the relationship they should develop between teaching and research (Austin, 1994). As noted above, some disciplinary cultures value teaching more than others. Faculty in a hard discipline in a college that predominantly values teaching may experience more tension around the relationship between teaching and research than a faculty member in a soft discipline in the same college. Conversely, faculty members in disciplines that place more value on teaching may feel conflicts if they are in universities that emphasize and heavily reward research. In sum, any consideration of departmental cultures, especially as they relate to the relationship between teaching and research, must take into account the larger context of the disciplinary and institutional cultures in which the department is placed.

Assessing Departmental and Institutional Cultures

Those interested in the relationship between teaching and research in a department or institution may want to examine the cultures of these units. For example, leaders may be interested in the values, behavioral norms, and assumptions about faculty work that characterize a particular department, or more broadly, a university or college. Exploring cultures is best done through the use of a variety of strategies, since any one method has inherent limitations (Austin, 1994; Baird, 1990). Qualitative methods are especially useful when one is seeking to learn how organizational members value, make sense of, and interpret their situations. Quantitative methods can be used to determine the extent of various perceptions. Through the use of a variety of assessment measures, a department chairperson, dean, institutional leader, or researcher can triangulate and compare information to develop a complex understanding of the culture of an organization or a department.

Two relatively straight-forward ways to assess a departmental or institutional culture are observation and listening. An observer interested in understanding how teaching and research relate in the culture might note which activities are rewarded, how faculty allocate their time, what they discuss with each other, the extent to which students are involved in research endeavors, and whether research issues are integrated into class discussions or assignments. Additionally, the symbols and rituals of the culture might be observed (Deal and

Kennedy, 1982), such as awards that the faculty value, the individuals who are held in especially high regard, and the special occasions through which faculty are honored. Closely related to observation is listening. In assessing a culture, one can strive to be a "cultural knower" (Bensimon, 1990, p. 83), listening to what faculty discuss and engaging them in conversation about their views of the department or institution. One might especially listen for faculty comments about their perceptions of the balance between teaching and research, about their beliefs and assumptions regarding the department or university values, and about their interpretation of the messages conveyed by various events, policies, rituals. The stories and myths they share can also be revealing.

In addition to observing and listening, which can happen daily and informally by anyone wishing to understand more about an organization's culture, one can use interviews and surveys. Interviews to ask explicitly about aspects of the culture—in this case, the relationship between teaching and research—can be carried out with individuals or groups and may involve either a structured protocol or open-ended, unstructured questions. A department interested in assessing its culture might schedule a retreat organized around a set of key questions to facilitate uninterrupted discussion about the culture. While analysis of culture typically relies on qualitative methods such as observation and interviewing, surveys can be useful in gathering data about perceptions of specific aspects of the culture. For example, a survey might include questions on the extent to which faculty engage in various behaviors that facilitate the integration of their research and teaching or items pertaining to the extent to which respondents agree with certain value statements.

While "climate" is a somewhat different construct than culture, pertaining more to members' views of various aspects of organizational life than to their embedded beliefs and values (Austin, 1994; Peterson and Spencer, 1990), the various quantitative and qualitative measures used by Volkwein and Carbone (1994) in assessing departmental research and teaching climates deserve mention. Their measures for research climate include number of grant applications and grants received in a department (quantitative measures), as well as deans' perceptions of the research climate and an expert panel's perceptions of the percentage of active scholars within a department (qualitative measure). Their measure for teaching climate includes number of faculty instructional contact hours and students' reports of number of out-of-class faculty-student academic contacts (quantitative measures), as well as deans' ratings of instructional climate and students' ratings of faculty interest in teaching within a department (qualitative measures).

In any formal assessment of a unit's culture, faculty members will want to know the purpose of the assessment, how any data collected through interviews or surveys will be used, and whether any views they express will be treated as confidential. If someone outside the unit or institution is conducting the exploration, he or she will have the advantage of seeing the culture with a fresh eye but will need to win the trust and respect of the faculty.

Approaches to Influencing Departmental and Institutional Cultures

Those who wish to understand or enter into the debate about the complementarity or conflict between teaching and research need to understand that issues of culture are important in this relationship. Institutions vary in their cultures, and departments each have their own cultural environment in which faculty negotiate the teaching-research relationship. Administrative and faculty leaders in some universities today are seeking ways to achieve greater balance between their research and teaching missions. However, cultures are not easy to change, since they involve deeply held values, beliefs, and assumptions. Those academic leaders who wish to encourage institutional and departmental cultures in which both teaching and research are valued, even if they are not fully complementary, may find the following strategies useful.

Reward Systems. Administrators who wish to encourage institutional and departmental cultures in which both teaching and research are valued must find ways to make reward systems more equitable. They may find the results of key studies on faculty rewards helpful. Faia (1976, p. 245) warns against "an unbalanced reward system" in which there are large disparities between the rewards for research productivity and the rewards for good teaching. Such an unbalanced reward system, he states, "may reduce role complementarity by, say, creating large disparities in the amount of time allocated to teaching and research, or by inculcating in professors a value system that gives short shrift to the responsibility for disseminating established knowledge." More recently, Fairweather (1993) has shown that, at all institutional types except liberal arts colleges, the more time faculty spend on teaching, the lower their pay. In all types of institutions, the more time they spend on research and the higher their publication rate, the greater their pay. He concludes that "teaching activity and productivity are at best neutral factors in pay, at worst negative predictors of pay" (p. 47). The implication seems clear. Reward systems should be more equitable.

Administrative Leadership. University and college leaders have important roles to play in affecting the cultures of their organizations. Their strategies must include both rhetoric and action. Astin and Chang (1995) have studied institutions that emphasize both research and teaching, as well as the factors related to such environments. They conclude that "in order to maintain a significant emphasis on both teaching and research, it appears necessary to effect somewhat of a compromise between the two" (p. 46). This advice parallels Fairweather's admonition (1993) that "academe must confront the difficult *tradeoffs* between teaching and research, and reconsider how best to encourage both teaching and research missions" (p. 47).

At universities and colleges striving for cultures that value both teaching and research, presidents, provosts, deans, and department chairpersons may need to articulate first that the institution or department indeed holds both endeavors to be important, and second, that high quality in both areas may involve, by necessity, not doing either activity at the same level as if it were the only mission. Institutional leaders also can show symbolically that they value both teaching and research by recognizing and honoring teaching accomplishments, as well as research accomplishments of faculty members, by providing resources for teaching activities (such as teaching-related conferences) as well as for research activities, and by articulating the teaching mission as clearly as the research mission.

Conversations and Networks. While teaching is a regular activity for most faculty members, they tend to discuss their thoughts and experiences regarding teaching less frequently than their ideas and progress concerning research. Institutions and departments that want to nurture cultures where both teaching and research are valued should consider how they are encouraging conversations about teaching and supporting networks of faculty that emerge around mutual teaching-related interests, as well as those around research projects. Faculty seminars and colloquia, monthly bag lunches, and teaching fellows programs to link new and experienced teachers are examples of the kinds of activities that contribute to cultural change toward greater valuing of teaching as well as research. Palmer (1993) has written that "good talk about good teaching"—conversations about autobiographical experiences in teaching, about critical moments in teaching practice, and about metaphors that serve as internal guides—sustain individual faculty members who are committed to teaching. Additionally, these kinds of conversations link individuals together with others of like mind, creating networks that slowly can change institutional and departmental cultures and their embedded values.

Policies and Practices. Institutional and departmental cultures also can be influenced through attention to such policies and practices as the socialization of new faculty, the allocation of resources for teaching as well as research excellence, and the availability of professional development opportunities for faculty interested in expanding their expertise as teachers. If leaders wish to change the culture of a university so that teaching and research are both valued, new faculty will need to receive consistent messages about the kind of work they are expected to do and the way in which the institution or department values both teaching and research. The kinds of activities for which they and others are rewarded is a particularly strong message to most junior faculty. When resources are directed to support the improvement of teaching as well as the development of research agendas and when regular professional development opportunities are available, such as funds for travel to teaching-related as well as research-oriented conferences and frequent on-campus seminars on teaching practice, the message is conveyed that both teaching and research merit the attention and support of the institution. Such policies and practices are useful tools in efforts to shift institutional and departmental cultures toward more equitable valuing of both teaching and research.

Concluding Thoughts

On a daily basis, faculty members work within the cultures of their disciplines, institutions, and departments. These cultures influence their approaches to their teaching and research and the relationship between activities in each of these areas. Any efforts to encourage faculty members to balance and relate their teaching and research in new ways will need to consider these academic cultures and their embedded values and norms.

References

Astin, A. W., and Chang, M. J. "Colleges that Emphasize Research and Teaching: Can You Have Your Cake and Eat It Too?" *Change*, 1995, 27 (5), 45–49.

Austin, A. E. "Faculty Cultures, Faculty Values." In W. G. Tierney (ed.), *Assessing Academic Climates and Cultures*. New Directions for Institutional Research, no. 68. San Francisco: Jossey-Bass, 1990.

Austin, A. E. "Faculty Cultures." In A. I. Morey (ed.), *The Encyclopedia of Higher Education*, Vol. 4. Elmsford, N.Y.: Pergamon Press, 1992.

Austin, A. E. "Understanding and Assessing Faculty Cultures and Climates." In M. K. Kinnick (ed.), *Providing Useful Information for Deans and Department Chairs*. New Directions for Institutional Research, no. 84. San Francisco: Jossey-Bass, 1994.

Baird, L. L. "Campus Climate: Using Surveys for Policy-Making and Understanding." In W. G. Tierney (ed.), *Assessing Academic Climates and Cultures*. New Directions for Institutional Research, no. 68. San Francisco: Jossey-Bass, 1990.

Becher, T. "Towards a Definition of Disciplinary Cultures." *Studies in Higher Education*, 1981, 6 (2), 109–122.

Becher, T. "The Cultural View." In B. R. Clark (ed.), *Perspectives on Higher Education: Eight Disciplinary and Comparative Views*. Los Angeles: University of California Press, 1984.

Becher, T. "The Disciplinary Shaping of the Profession." In B. R. Clark (ed.), *The Academic Profession: National, Disciplinary, and Institutional Settings*. Los Angeles: University of California Press, 1987.

Bensimon, E. M. "The New President and Understanding the Campus." In W. G. Tierney (ed.), *Assessing Academic Climates and Cultures*. New Directions for Institutional Research, no. 68. San Francisco: Jossey-Bass, 1990.

Bergquist, W. H. *The Four Cultures of the Academy: Insights and Strategies for Improving Leadership in Collegiate Organizations*. San Francisco: Jossey-Bass, 1992.

Biglan, A. "The Characteristics of Subject Matter in Different Academic Areas." *Journal of Applied Psychology*, 1973, 57 (3), 195–203.

Braxton, J. M. "Affinity Disciplines and the Improvement of Undergraduate Education." In M. Marincovich and N. Hativa (eds.), *Disciplinary Differences in Teaching and Learning in Higher Education*. New Directions for Teaching and Learning. San Francisco: Jossey-Bass, 1996.

Braxton, J. M., and Hargens, L. L. "Variation Among Academic Disciplines: Analytical Frameworks and Research." In J. C. Smart (ed.), *Higher Education: Handbook of Theory and Research, Vol. XI*. New York: Agathon Press, 1996.

Clark, B. R. *The Higher Education System: Academic Organization in Cross-National Perspective*. Los Angeles: University of California Press, 1984.

Clark, B. R. "Listening to the Professoriate." *Change*, 1985, 17 (5), 36–43.

Clark, B. R. *The Academic Life: Small Worlds, Different Worlds*. Princeton, N.J.: Carnegie Foundation for the Advancement of Teaching, 1987.

Deal, T. E., and Kennedy, A. A. *Corporate Cultures: The Rites and Rituals of Corporate Life.* Reading, Mass.: Addison-Wesley, 1982.

Faia, M. A. "Teaching and Research: Rapport or Mesalliance." *Research in Higher Education,* 1976, *4,* 235–246.

Fairweather, J. S. "Faculty Rewards Reconsidered: The Nature of Tradeoffs." *Change,* 1993, *25* (4), 44–47.

Feldman, K. A. "Research Productivity and Scholarly Accomplishment of College Teachers as Related to Their Instructional Effectiveness: A Review and Exploration." *Research in Higher Education,* 1987, *26,* 227–298.

Geertz, C. *The Interpretation of Cultures.* New York: Basic Books, 1973.

Kuh, G. D., and Whitt, E. J. *The Invisible Tapestry: Culture in American Colleges and Universities.* ASHE-ERIC Higher Education Report No. 1. Washington, D.C.: Association for the Study of Higher Education, 1988.

Light, W., Jr., Marsden, L. R., and Corl, T. C. *The Impact of the Academic Revolution on Faculty Careers.* AAHE-ERIC Higher Education Report No. 10. Washington, D.C.: American Association of Higher Education, 1972.

Lodahl, J. B., and Gordon, G.G. "The Structure of Scientific Fields and the Functioning of University Graduate Departments." *American Sociological Review,* 1972, 37 (1), 57–72.

Palmer, P. J. "Good Talk about Good Teaching: Improving Teaching through Conversation." *Change,* 1993, 25 (6), 8–13.

Peterson, M. W., Cameron, K. S., Mets, L. A., Jones, P., and Ettington, D. *The Organizational Context for Teaching and Learning: A Review of the Research Literature.* Ann Arbor: National Center for Research to Improve Postsecondary Teaching and Learning, University of Michigan, 1986.

Peterson, M. W., and Spencer, M. G. "Understanding Academic Culture and Climate." In W. G. Tierney (ed.), *Assessing Academic Climates and Cultures.* New Directions for Institutional Research, no. 68. San Francisco: Jossey-Bass, 1990.

Ruscio, K. P. "Many Sectors, Many Professions." In B. R. Lark (ed.), *The Academic Profession: National, Disciplinary, and Institutional Settings.* Los Angeles: University of California Press, 1987.

Schein, E. H. *Organizational Culture and Leadership: A Dynamic View.* San Francisco: Jossey-Bass, 1985.

Volkwein, J. F., and Carbone, D. A. "The Impact of Departmental Research and Teaching Climates on Undergraduate Growth and Satisfaction." *The Journal of Higher Education,* 1994, 65 (2), 147–167.

ANN E. AUSTIN is associate professor and coordinator of the Higher, Adult, and Lifelong Education Program at Michigan State University, East Lansing, Michigan.

The debate about faculty roles is addressed by questioning the debate itself. The author suggests a way to change the public conversation about faculty by changing the descriptions of what faculty do and the research approach to studying it. She argues that a holistic perspective on faculty is necessary as a starting point for policy-relevant research.

Framing the Public Policy Debate on Faculty: What Is the Role of Research?

Meredith Jane Ludwig

Policy makers look for simple, bottom-line answers to complex questions, reflecting the policy arena in which they work and the public's interest. Sometimes these questions are raised by the policy makers themselves, but often they emerge from the writings of journalists, members of the academic community, and members of the public. Regardless of the origin, the questions are often expressed simply, but they are not simple to answer. To gather the evidence required to solve the policy problem usually would involve sophisticated research and analysis. For higher education, the most celebrated of these questions have been:

- What is the meaning of a college degree?
- Why does it take students so much longer to graduate from college these days?
- Why does the cost of college keep going up?
- What do faculty do?

The answers to such questions go to the heart of what higher education is all about—what it does with its financial and human resources, what its impact is on the participants, and how all of this happens within the larger socio-political-economic environment. Further, the answers to the questions provided by many research studies and commission reports have had profound policy implications for colleges and universities and are likely to continue to influence how higher education does its work. This *New Directions* volume focuses on the last question in this list, but in addressing it, cannot escape the overlapping issues embedded in the others.

When policy-relevant questions are raised, who provides the answers? Research has always played an important part in this process of examination. At the national level, the support of the first commissioner of education for a system of accountability for education signaled over 120 years of collecting and reporting on the condition of education (U.S. Department of Education, 1994). Commissions have been the hallmark of the American process of decision making about education (Orenstein and Levine, 1989). Until recently, most lawmakers and administrators were willing to wait for thorough studies, even longitudinal ones, that examined large and important policy questions, for example, whether Head Start meets congressional goals for economically disadvantaged students.

In the current political climate, however, patience is not long. Since the reauthorization of the Higher Education Act in 1992, the focus on assessment and program improvement in higher education (an internally controlled process) has shifted to that of accountability (an externally controlled process). These movements have resulted in more or less regulation for colleges and universities, as much of this effort deflated in the past year, under the political themes of regulatory relief, devolution of authority, and clearly defined public benefits (Ewell, 1995).

Peter Ewell has written about this period of history from 1992–1995: "The bottom line is that the question of establishing acceptable minimum performance thresholds on core institutional outcomes has been raised publicly and politically for the first time in every state" (1995, p. 15).). The responsibility of faculty for the student share of institutional outcomes has been clearly stated by government leaders, by prominent educators, and is felt keenly by many faculty themselves (Ewell, 1994). This responsibility is to teach.

Much research addresses the policy question of faculty responsibility by pointing to the relationship between research and teaching activities. This focus seeks a helpful resolution to the academy's debate about the relationship between research and teaching. It seeks to demonstrate that both activities have the potential to strengthen the work of faculty overall, improve the intellectual environment for faculty, and contribute to student achievement. However, interviews with legislators, trustee representatives, and students indicate that this may be an inefficient use of the time and knowledge of experienced researchers. The public and its representatives are not interested in the academic side of this issue (Portch, 1993; Pratt, 1993; Ewell, 1994). Considering the lack of understanding among the public about academic research and its relevance, an academic conversation about the question of roles may, in itself, be a barrier to improving the understanding sought by higher education of the faculty contribution. In fact, it is time to consider whether this debate is indeed a false one—a point at which this chapter begins.

A False Debate About Faculty Work

How did the policy debate on faculty work emerge and gain such a high profile in the 1990s? A series of books in the early 1990s described the faculty in the higher education academy as "spoiled, devious, and venal" (Winston, 1994,

p. 9). The notion that faculty were not doing what they were supposed to be doing and were, in fact, misrepresenting themselves, was a familiar theme in these writings. Perhaps the most famous book sounding the theme of misrepresentation was *ProfScam* by Charles Sykes (1988). The criticism of faculty work was also given some underlying support through the academic research of William Massy and Robert Zemsky (1992), who described the entrepreneurial conditions that existed in some academic departments of higher education institutions, where the faculty reward system led to "increases in discretionary time," "higher instructional costs all around" and "reduced attention to undergraduates and teaching" (Winston, 1994). Analyses of the National Survey of Postsecondary Faculty showed that faculty whose research activities consumed more of their time than teaching were rewarded by higher salaries, and the publicity that ensued extended the general perception that faculty not only did research because they liked it but their cultural mores reinforced this behavior and needed to be changed.

Once researchers and writers raised the question of the accountability of faculty for student outcomes, the public's representatives took it to the level of a policy concern. Disparities between the public's and the academic community's perceptions of faculty work led to state-by-state policies regarding the quantification of faculty productivity. In some states and at some institutions, the results have led to a set of policies seeking to control faculty time to ensure that it is devoted to teaching.

The results of years of previous research on faculty as individuals, as members of different departments, as part of different sectors of institutions form an impressive body of knowledge. However, as a number of higher education writers and educational researchers confirm, this knowledge has not had an impact on the public policy debate about faculty (Peters, 1994). Instead, it is almost as if the policy makers chose to disregard the knowledge gained as understanding for what faculty do, in lieu of a more useful focus on student contact hours. According to Layzell (1990), higher education research does not influence administrators who make policy because of a lack of focus on "pressing problems" and an emphasis on methodology, narrowly framed studies, and overly technical presentation of results.

Ewell blames a communication gap for the continuing policy debate about what faculty should do. He has pinpointed four areas where a communication gap has been created because of a difference in the way higher education hears what the public says or asks of it. I paraphrase Ewell's (1994) "script" of this mismatched conversation as follows:

- When the public message is that there is no more money for higher education, higher education refuses to believe it.
- When the public asks higher education to change how it does its work, higher education insists the quality will be sacrificed and does not respond with flexibility and innovation.

- When the public says the bottom line is students are not getting what they need, higher education faculty defend their work and say they are being accused unfairly of not working hard enough.
- When the public and its representatives ask higher education institutions to take responsibility for what they do, higher education views it as a statement of mistrust and an intention of micromanagement.

Ewell says the expectations of the public and policy makers about the fundamental work of faculty are not misguided, nor do they indicate the existence of a misunderstanding about what faculty should do. The problem, he suggests, has been created by the academy itself, because it has interpreted these expectations of faculty as the age-old debate about research versus teaching. This take on the public's concern is "largely unproductive," as he explains:

> For the vast majority of policymakers, higher education is (and should be) over-whelmingly about teaching—and in particular, undergraduate teaching. Current discussions about reshaping scholarship, regardless of how important they appear to us, will have little resonance for those on the outside unless their results are made visible in a classroom, student lab assignment, or hallway conversation. [Ewell, 1994, p. 4]

Ewell's suggestion that the debate is unproductive is, I believe, a novel one. Most of us, in our own writings and research, have sustained the debate, all the while proclaiming we are trying to settle it. Maybe we should stop having it. The debate interests us, and it absorbs our intellectual attention, but is it keeping us from considering the real question?

Perhaps higher education can contribute to the public's interest in its outcomes by making it first clear what these activities are.

For example, Ewell (1994) points out that there is a lack of understanding among the public or in the state legislatures about what conducting research means. The public generally hears about the findings of discipline-based academic research through the media—newspapers, popular magazines, and television. It is asked to make sense of these findings by putting them into one of two categories: (1) an interesting statistic to be taken out and cited as needed or (2) research results that may or may not have a direct impact on the quality of life. In both cases, partly due to journalistic ethics and partly due to the nature of the statistical findings, the public is cautioned about the use or the reliance on the information at this time. Researchers are questioned about the motives behind their choice of subject and the origin of resources that allow the studies to take place. It is not difficult then to understand why reports from the annual meetings of scholarly societies are not meaningful to most members of the public.

In general, the contributions of discipline-based scholarship are largely enigmatic to the public. A clear exception to this phenomenon is the awarding of the Nobel Prizes. When the ground-breaking work of these scientists, humanists, and peace makers is noted, it is within a time frame that makes sense to the public and affirms the contribution to the public good.

There are many explanations in the higher education literature for the existence of this gap in understanding about research and its relevance to the public. Schon (1995) locates the origins in the epistemology of the research university, saying faculty and institutional choices made between the principles of "rigor and relevance" have led to a splitting of academic focus away from the practical problems around which human activity (including teaching) is focused. Not only faculty but also researchers studying faculty have accepted this split focus, and thus our explanations of what faculty do sustain the public's feeling that it has little relevance to their lives.

Schon's solution is to put our epistemological house in order. If we are going to talk about a new kind of scholarship, he says, we need to establish the institutional structure that supports it. In other words, it "must make room for the practitioner's reflection in and on action" (1995, p. 34).

Legislators may be inclined to agree with what is essentially a more practical orientation to faculty responsibilities. In recent interviews with two Virginia legislators, faculty were exhorted to do some "self-analysis." These public representatives were not referring to the customary academic introspection. They insisted that faculty need to "come to grips with the realities of our world today" (Pratt, 1993, p. 17). Layzell and others suggest a way to address both the public lack of understanding and the legislative wake-up call, and that is to conceive of faculty as an asset to the community and to the state, in its economic and social goals for its citizens, and to apply their competencies and skills accordingly (1996). These messages about the practical orientation of academic research are coming very close to a new conceptualization of the way we do and talk about academic research, or as Schon refers to it "action research" (1995).

Determining the essence of teaching is a slightly different but still problematic case, because most of the public shares a common yet limited conception about it. Riordan (1993) supports the notion that the language in the debate is constricting our progress in understanding and resolving the researcher-teacher debate. He asks if even the word "teaching" is too limiting because of the image it projects; he suggests that searching for the essence of what is teaching will lead to "the most fruitful path of inquiry in considering the nature of scholarship" (1993, p. 1). Riordan's new direction for teaching is to be found in making it the center of one's scholarly studies. This might help answer the public's questions about the relevance of academic research, because the public would understand the idea of conducting research on one's own teaching, especially if it has a direct influence on the outcomes for students (Ewell's "I can see it in the classroom" kind of evidence). Like Ewell, Riordan contends that student learning is the ultimate goal of what faculty do. Therefore, faculty scholarship should be conceived of as activity that is grounded in the questions that help faculty connect students to the processes of their discipline and to other disciplines as appropriate. The ultimate test of the usefulness of a discipline is when students can make use of it as a frame-work in their own lives.

A number of faculty across the country are involved in scholarship about teaching, as reported in the monthly publications of the American Association for Higher Education. A recent article by Schon (1995) about this "new schol-arship" for example, seems to me to sum up Wilson's and Riordan's reflective inquiry about their own teaching and scholarship.

Schon calls the reflective work done by practitioners "knowing in action." This description of doing work implies that we are knowledgeable in a special way about what we do. When we act, we not only apply that knowledge with-out thinking about it, we are constantly reevaluating that knowledge and devel-oping new knowledge about our action. Schon calls this "action research," and it is as applicable for the physician, as it is for the business manager or the fac-ulty member. Thus, if we take Schon's theoretical perspective as a jumping-off point, we must be prepared to look at the job of faculty in a more objective and holistic way. It is a job, like any other. Schon's perspective also points to a way of undertaking research about faculty work focusing on the relevance of that work. The question is, can research take such a concept as a starting point and fashion a new direction to help the public understand the job of faculty? In the next section of this chapter, I describe how to begin that task.

Accumulation and Reflection:
Design Inquiry Applied to the Study of Faculty

Higher education has learned the hard way that a tradition of academic research has not been successful in answering the public and policy makers' questions about faculty responsibility. Neither has the current way of studying faculty productivity. In fact, some say going down this path will continue to lead higher education in the wrong direction.

In the 1990s, administrators, legislators, and coordinating and governing boards directed research and planning staff at institutions and organizations to document what faculty did with their time. The outcomes of these trends have been beneficial for researchers to some extent, for example, they have led to the development of systematic methodologies and a broader dissemination of information about faculty. However, these approaches to studying faculty have been limited by their situation in a traditional starting point for explicating fac-ulty work. Thus, the public perception about the job of faculty and the rele-vance of faculty work has not been changed.

Layzell and others offer a good description of the problems inherent in relying on productivity analysis to describe the work of faculty (1996). First, to measure productivity "in its entirety" means identifying the "tangible" and "intangible" inputs and outputs of higher education. Since measuring the intangibles is difficult, the researcher ends by sacrificing the element of "qual-ity" that is a component in either input or output. Second, faculty productiv-ity is often the result of a combined effort with other faculty and with students.

The effect of this combined effort is not always easy to isolate from the product itself. Third, workload is not equivalent to what faculty do, thus cannot be used by itself to describe productivity (1996).

The conceptual problems Layzell and others identify are traceable to the predilection of researchers to start from the wrong scientific paradigm to answer the question. Researchers who study faculty would do well to consider the characteristics of the evidence they are seeking before they begin their research. Peters writes there are two types of evidence, "narrative" (literary, intuitive, and interpretive) versus "paradigmatic" (scientific, objective, and logical). We tend to rely on the paradigmatic (Peters, 1994). According to Saunders (1996), "The paradigm of the physical sciences leads us to believe there is a strict connection between the knowledge we gain from our research on a physical system and our capacity to manipulate the natural or human worlds" (p. 129). Solutions are easier to imagine and develop, claims Saunders (1996), whereas:

> In hermeneutic fields such as those involved in determining meaning, problems, solutions and research present themselves as unrelated texts which do not coalesce into a practical means to manipulate social nature. Thus knowing the demographic statistics of our faculty may not help us defend against a charge that we discriminated against a group just as knowing the law does not guarantee a lawyer will win his or her case.
>
> I propose that we replace this focus on faculty productivity that is driving the research we do with an approach that is characterized by "accumulation and reflection." This is distinctively narrative rather than paradigmatic. How then do we collect data that are narrative rather than paradigmatic? Essayist Barbara Kingsolver writes of the methods of the natural historians of the nineteenth century, Charles Darwin and Henry David Thoreau. For example, while not advocating we go back to the state of knowledge of those times, she notes Darwin's straightforward and simple view that theory can be developed by accumulating data and reflecting on it (Kingsolver, 1995).
>
> Thoreau took this advice to accumulate and reflect and moved "toward an articulation of unifying principles," a process of generalization that allowed him the time and reflective imagination to start with "a clump of seeds caught in the end of a cow's whisking tail" and to "wonder (ed) enviously what finds were presenting themselves to the laborers picking wool in nearby factories" (Kingsolver, 1995, p. 241). Kingsolver writes that "Thoreau understood that the scientist and the science are inseparable" (1995, p. 239).

This I believe is also Schon's (1995) message in his notion of "design inquiry." He starts with the conception of "Deweyan inquiry," a process he describes as studying "situations that are problematic—that are confusing, uncertain, or conflicted, and block the free flow of action."

> The inquirer is in, and in transaction with, the problematic situation. He or she must construct the meaning and frame the problem of the situation, thereby

setting the stage for problem-solving, which in combination with changes in
the external context, brings a new problematic situation into being. [p. 31]

Schon is encouraging educational institutions to regard the principal work
of faculty to be the designers of inquiry, a kind of melding of practice and
research that he calls "action research" and that begins with problems and uni-
fies the "scientist with the science," as Kingsolver has written of Thoreau. This
vision of faculty work brings the knower and the known-unknown together.
It supplants the traditional notions of division of faculty work by assuming the
practitioner has specialized knowledge about teaching, research, and service
and that all of these come together in the process of being faculty. It welcomes
the view that faculty work is evolving and fundamentally grounded in student
learning and in faculty development. It also offers us, as researchers, a way to
orient ourselves to the authentic description of faculty work.

An important recommendation emerging from Schon's theoretical model
is that researchers should be partners with the key investigators—the faculty
themselves. Schon describes his own efforts to encourage the role of faculty in
conducting action research on their own design inquiry. In Schon's example, a
faculty member was unsuccessful in convincing his peers of the contribution
of his work during a process of evaluation and tenure review when he lacked
data on what students had learned and the relevance of his development work
to his discipline. Studying the process of design inquiry would have led to such
evidence, important knowledge that could then have reinforced additional
inquiry. It also would have given administrators information about the excep-
tional quality of the faculty product. Schon's conclusion (supported by teaching development specialists): Faculty must document the processes through
which they design settings of inquiry for themselves, for their students, and
for their colleagues (Schon, 1995; Hutchings, 1995).

Conclusion: The Changing Responsibilities
of Those Engaged in the Policy Debate

This chapter began by stating the public policy question about faculty, then
questioning the question itself. I showed how, by pursuing a scientific, paradigmatic approach to the study of faculty work, we have maintained the false
debate that faculty work is divided. Finally, I suggest a three-stage approach to
remedying the situation into which we have led ourselves. I suggest a new
direction for researchers in studying who faculty are and what they do, with
an emphasis on the accumulation of data and reflection on that data.

Research and faculty together can create the capacity needed to answer
the academy's questions of itself and the public's questions about faculty.
Change is needed in two areas.

First, we must recognize that by continuing the research tradition of look-
ing at faculty in the same fragmented way, we are sustaining the view that their
work activities are not integrated and leaving open the door to the academic

debate that the work they do conflicts with the needs of students and the expectations of the public.

Second, by adopting a "sound bite" approach to policy-relevant research, we are keeping ourselves as researchers from engaging a naturalistic design inquiry that fits better with the study of the intellectual lives of practitioners.

We need a change in the way we describe faculty and a change in the research approach we use to document what faculty do. Then we will be able to change the public conversation about faculty.

The new direction I propose combines the changes in faculty description and in policy-relevant research to attend to Layzell's (1990) three criticisms of research vis-à-vis policy questions: a lack of focus on pressing problems, an emphasis on methodology and narrowly framed studies, and an overly technical presentation of results. In their publication exploring the theory and practice of policy analysis, Gill and Saunders describe a model developed by Cates (1979, p. 528, cited in Gill and Saunders, 1992, p. 11). To respond to the kind of environment in which higher education policy is made, policy analysis must acknowledge the "changing conditions" or frequent "changes in policy direction." Not only do the external questions change, higher education observers can be quite quixotic. Policy that affects the way higher education does its business may emerge, for example, suddenly from the U.S. Congress and the federal government in response to what they see as the pressing problems—recently of loan defaults. How can higher education respond to such a chaotic policy environment and maintain some stability on behalf of the students it serves? To respond, Cates's model advances the idea that "the criteria for good policy is [sic] a restructuring of the problem so that new solutions are found" (1979, p. 11). Gill and Saunders (1992) describe this as a model based on creativity, and the new criterion for good policy is that "the policy analysis values are intuition, innovation, change, ambiguity, and risk" (p. 11).

The design inquiry model supports a change for researchers and policy analysts by putting into operation three stages of research activity: *description, accumulation,* and *reflection.*

Description. To discover what faculty do, we need a more holistic framework that takes into consideration the individualistic nature of faculty work. This framework must acknowledge that the landscape of faculty will change based on the climate in and around the institution and the way faculty define themselves—their peer group affinities, their interactions with students, and with colleagues and other communities.

Accumulation of data. Faculty and researchers must work together to assemble both process and product descriptions of what faculty do. This accumulation of data takes time and requires patience. However, it has significant payoffs. It will allow the illumination of the design inquiry process that is the life of faculty. It will allow researchers to point to the focus of faculty on real, pressing problems. It argues for broadening the methods used to study faculty, rather than narrowing them. Finally, without it, we will not be able to formulate the generalizations we seek, either about faculty or about their accomplishments.

Reflection. To describe what faculty do, researchers must also engage in reflective inquiry. We must study the knowledge we have about research and teaching and bring that to bear on what we see faculty are doing. Our reflection is enriched if we consider what is known about faculty and what knowledge is sought about faculty.

This approach to studying faculty must be based on a more holistic description of faculty—one that acknowledges faculty work as evolving and embedded in students' learning.

The information we need to communicate about faculty is not always consistent, not always available; and we do not always ask the right questions. If we pay close attention to the data needs of our audiences and our relationships with those who report on faculty work, as researchers we can change the direction of our conversation, reformulate the questions about faculty, and ultimately communicate in new ways about the intellectual life and contributions of faculty. Faculty must be convinced they are essential to this research and can gain from it. Faculty need to be active participants in research on their lives.

The result of our efforts should be a better relationship between research and policy, not a reformulation of what faculty do. The faculty "essence" may remain a bit mysterious using this approach. However, according to scholars like Bensimon (1996) and Schon (1995), this conception of faculty as practitioners is closer to what is relevant and what is real than the artificial conception we have created in the public's mind of researcher/teacher/public servant.

References

Bensimon, E. "Faculty Identity: Essential, Imposed, or Constructed?" In *Integrating Research on Faculty: Seeking New Ways to Communicate About the Academic Life of Faculty.* Washington, D.C.: U.S. Department of Education, Office of Educational Research and Improvement, National Center for Education Statistics, March 1996.

Cates, C. "Beyond Muddling: Creativity." *Public Administration Review,* 1979, 39 (6), 527–532.

Ewell, P. T. "The Neglected Art of Collective Responsibility: Restoring Our Links With Society." Commissioned paper for the American Association for Higher Education Forum on Faculty Roles and Rewards Second National Conference, New Orleans, January 1994.

Ewell, P. T. "From the States, Acting Out Postsecondary Reviews." *Assessment Update,* 1995, 7 (1), 14.

Ewell, P. T. "From the States, So Are They Really Going Away?" *Assessment Update,* 1995, 7 (4), 8.

Gill, J. I., and Saunders, L. (eds.). *Developing Effective Policy Analysis in Higher Education.* New Directions for Institutional Research, no. 76. San Francisco: Jossey-Bass, 1992.

Hutchings, P. "From Results to Reflective Practice." *Assessment Update,* January-February 1995.

Kingsolver, B. "The Forest in the Seeds." *High Tide in Tucson.* New York: HarperCollins, 1995, 236–242.

Layzell, D. T. "Most Research on Higher Education is Stale, Irrelevant, and of Little Use to Policy Makers." *Chronicle of Higher Education,* October 24, 1990, B1-B3.

Layzell, D. T., Lovell, C. D., and Gill, J. I. "Developing Faculty as an Asset in a Period of Change and Uncertainty." In *Integrating Research on Faculty: Seeking New Ways to Communicate About the Academic Life of Faculty*. Washington, D.C.: U.S. Department of Education, Office of Educational Research and Improvement, National Center for Education Statistics, March 1996.

Ludwig, M. "Accountability Reporting." *Report of the States*. Washington, D.C.: American Association of State Colleges and Universities, 1995.

Massy, W. F., and Zemsky, R. "Faculty Discretionary Time: Departments and the 'Academic Ratchet.'" Stanford Institute of Higher Education Research, Discussion Paper 4, May 1992.

Orenstein, A. and Levine, D. *Foundations of Education*. Boston: Houghton Mifflin, 1989.

Peters, R. "Accountability and the End(s) of Higher Education." *Change*, November/December 1994, 16–23.

Portch, S. R. "Friends or Foe?" *AAHE Bulletin*, November 1993, 11–20.

Pratt, A. M. "Public Perceptions, Public Policy." *AAHE Bulletin*, November 1993, 15–17.

Riordan, T. "Beyond the Debate: The Nature of Teaching." Paper presented at the annual meeting of the American Educational Research Association, Atlanta, April 1993.

Saunders, L. "Prospects for Integrating Research on Higher Education Faculty." In *Integrating Research on Faculty: Seeking New Ways to Communicate About the Academic Life of Faculty*. Washington, D.C.: U.S. Department of Education, Office of Educational Research and Improvement, National Center for Education Statistics, March 1996.

Schon, D. A. "The New Scholarship Requires A New Epistemology." *Change*, November/December 1995, 27–34.

Sykes, C. J. *ProfScam: Professors and the Demise of Higher Education*. Washington, D.C.: Regnery Gateway, 1988.

U.S. Department of Education. Office of Educational Research and Improvement. National Center for Education Statistics. *The Condition of Education*, 1994.

Winkler, A. M. "The Faculty Workload Question." *Change*, July/August 1992, 36–41.

Winston, G. C. "The Decline in Undergraduate Teaching." *Change*, October 1994, 9–15.

MEREDITH JANE LUDWIG *is director of the Office of Association Research at the American Association of State Colleges and Universities in Washington, D.C. She also teaches on perspectives on American education to master's-level students in the secondary education program at the George Washington University Graduate School of Education and Human Development.*

*The authors summarize points made in the volume and conclude
that, with few exceptions, research activity does not hinder faculty
from meeting the educational needs of students as clients of
undergraduate college teaching. They also offer recommendations
for practice and research.*

Public Trust, Research Activity, and the Ideal of Service to Students as Clients of Teaching

John M. Braxton, Joseph B. Berger

The American public generally believes that undergraduate teaching is the faculty's primary responsibility (Ewell, 1994). The public also perceives that faculty research activity is detrimental to undergraduate teaching (Volkwein and Carbone, 1994). As a consequence, public policy makers have become increasingly concerned about what faculty do (see Chapter Eight). Such a concern has resulted in state policies requiring the measurement of faculty productivity. In some states, policies that control faculty time devoted to teaching reflect this concern.

Such policies represent efforts by public policy makers to exercise social control over faculty role performance. Society grants colleges and faculty members autonomy in carrying out their professional responsibilities in exchange for adherence to the ideal of service (Goode, 1969; Braxton, 1986). The service ideal dictates that professionals serve the needs of clients and that the professional rather than the client determines what these needs are (Goode, 1969). Faculty research activity violates this service ideal when it diverts professionals from serving their students, and consequently, the public loses trust and attempts to exert social control.

Ludwig (in Chapter Eight) cogently argues that questions concerning the relationship between teaching and research incorrectly specify the nature of the public's concern. However, faculty members, academic administrators, and college and university presidents need to know whether the research activities of faculty do, in fact, unfavorably affect the welfare of students as clients. Like teaching, research activity also has its advocates (Turner, 1990).

Turner describes the evolution of research in America as a form of patronage system that has created a complex web of relationships, distributions of discretion, knowledge, and trust. This patronage system has resulted in world leadership in knowledge production in most fields for the United States (Newman, 1985a, 1985b). Viewing the American public as patrons of modern scholarship reframes the discussion about how faculty spend their time. Such discussion is important because we need to know whether or not research activity diminishes the quality of teaching.

Research Activity and Client Welfare

Such dimensions of teaching as course content, norms pertaining to relationships between faculty and students, student-faculty interactions, classroom practices, effective teaching behaviors, and student cognitive development entail professional choices by faculty that either directly or indirectly address the needs of students as learners. Faculty choices concerning these dimensions of college teaching require adherence to the ideal of service to college students as clients; students as individuals (Blau, 1973) or as members of groups (Schein, 1972) are clients of teaching. Does faculty research activity negatively affect those clients?

Course Content. Effective functioning as an adult in contemporary society depends to some extent on familiarity with current scholarship in a variety of academic disciplines. Client service requires the transmission of current scholarship to students.

Current scholarship in an academic discipline can be conveyed through the assignment of current journal articles and supplemental course reading, through the assignment of current scholarly books and supplemental reading, and through lecturing on topics from current journal articles and current scholarly books. Research indicates that these activities are performed to a greater extent by faculty who publish a great deal than by faculty who seldom or never publish (Braxton, 1983). Thus, research activity serves students as clients through the transmission of current scholarship.

Norms as Guides to Teaching Behavior. Most college and university faculty have considerable autonomy in how they perform the teaching role (Braxton, Bayer, and Finkelstein, 1992). Consequently, informal mechanisms of social control that provide guides to appropriate and inappropriate behavior with respect to clients are needed (Goode, 1957). Norms function as such mechanisms of social control.

Norms delineating inappropriate behaviors in college teaching are: *interpersonal disregard, particularistic grading, moral turpitude,* and *inadequate planning* (Braxton, Bayer, and Finkelstein, 1992). If faculty engage in these behaviors, the effect would be detrimental to the social context of classes and student learning (Braxton, Bayer, and Finkelstein, 1992). However, Sullivan (Chapter Two) finds that faculty research activity does not affect the espousal of each of these four norms by college and university faculty members. Hence, extensive involvement in research by faculty apparently does not jeopardize the welfare of students as clients.

Student-Faculty Interactions. Faculty interactions with students positively influence students' intellectual development and academic achievement (Pascarella, 1980; Sorcinelli, 1991). If faculty are unwilling to be accessible to students and interact with them, then student learning may be impaired and the ideal of service compromised.

The authors of Chapter Three showed that prolific scholars espouse favorable attitudes toward their accessibility to students, whereas those who publish less are not as likely to do so. Moreover, in Chapter Four, Olsen and Simmons assert that frequent publishers are not any less likely to encourage contact with students in and outside of class than are faculty who seldom or never publish. The authors also report that although prolific scholars do not differ from their less-prolific colleagues in the number of formal office hours per week, they do report a lower percentage of students in lower level courses taking advantage of their office hours, and they report knowing their students as individuals. However, faculty with high levels of publication productivity do not differ from their less-productive counterparts in the amount of contact they have with students who are experiencing course difficulty and in the percentage of students in upper level courses who come to office hours.

Classroom Practices. Classroom practices affecting the interests of students as clients include instruction and the assessment of student academic performance—practices that influence student learning.

Olsen and Simmons also contend (Chapter Four) that faculty can select various instructional approaches that ensure personal efficiency at the expense of instructional effectiveness, approaches that include not teaching 100- and 200-level courses, using lecture rather than discussion as the primary mode of instruction, and not requiring papers in 100- and 200-level courses. However, the authors found little evidence that faculty who publish a great deal are any more inclined to choose instructional approaches ensuring personal efficiency than are faculty who are moderate or infrequent publishers.

Client welfare also entails the assessment of student course performance. Course examinations, term papers, and other written exercises provide media for the assessment of student course performance. These course-level academic processes also index the level of academic demands or rigor expected of students (Braxton and Nordvall, 1985; Braxton, 1993; Nordvall and Braxton, forthcoming). Academic rigor manifests itself in examination questions and written exercises through the level of understanding of course content required by these processes. Questions or assignments calling for the recall or recognition of course content—knowledge level—require a lower level of understanding than do questions requiring critical thinking (Braxton and Nordvall, 1985; Braxton, 1992; Nordvall and Braxton, forthcoming).

In Chapter Five, Johnson addresses the relationship between faculty research activity and the rigor of the examinations they give. Assuming that greater course rigor represents the best interests of students as clients, research activity leads to mixed results. Faculty who produce more articles ask more knowledge-level examination questions and fewer critical thinking questions than do their colleagues who publish fewer articles. In contrast, research activity viewed as book productivity enhances academic rigor, since academics who publish scholarly books ask more critical thinking examination questions than do individuals who have not published a book in the last three years.

Effective Teaching. Effective teaching involves the use of good teaching practices, which, in turn, affect student learning. Chickering and Gamson (1987) identify the following principles of good teaching practice: encouragement of cooperation among students, encouragement of active learning, giving of prompt feedback, emphasizing time on task, communicating high expectation, and respecting diverse talents and ways of learning. Because research shows that faculty adherence to these principles enhances student learning (Sorcinelli, 1991), noncompliance with these principles negatively affects the welfare of students as clients.

In Chapter Four, Olsen and Simmons demonstrate that heavy involvement in research does not detrimentally influence adherence to five of these good teaching practices. Prolific scholars differ little from their less-published colleagues on their espousal of such good teaching practices as encouraging cooperation among students, emphasizing time on task, communicating high expectations, respecting diverse talents and ways of learning, and encouraging active learning. However, faculty with records of high publication productivity are less apt to give their students prompt feedback on course assignments than are their moderate- and low-publishing counterparts.

Student course ratings offer another approach to appraising teaching effectiveness. Because student course ratings are positively associated with course achievement (Cohen, 1981), they offer a valid indicator of teaching effectiveness.

Extensive research activity does not compromise teaching effectiveness, as indexed in student course ratings. In eighteen of thirty studies, research activity wields little or no influence on student assessment of teaching effectiveness, whereas it exerts a positive effect on teaching effectiveness in eleven of thirty studies (Braxton, Chapter One). Thus, scholars involved in research are attentive to the welfare of their students as clients of teaching role performance.

Student Cognitive Development. The cognitive development of students is fundamental to their well-being as college and university clients. Cognitive development includes both knowledge acquisition and the development of intellectual skills and values (Pascarella and Terenzini, 1991).

Only indirect evidence exists about the relationship between research activity and student learning. In Chapter Six, Gavlick posits a possible link between research activity and student course achievement. He postulates that research activity leads to the enactment of teaching behaviors which, in turn, positively influence student course achievement. This link is grounded in research on the relationship between scholarly activity and various teaching behaviors (Feldman, 1987) and the influence of various teaching behaviors on student course achievement (Cohen, 1981). Research testing Gavlick's proposed link will help us determine whether scholarly activity enhances or impedes student knowledge acquisition.

However, firmer evidence regarding perceived intellectual growth exists. Volkwein and Carbone (1994) report that departments having climates marked by excellence in both teaching and research wield a greater influence on students' perceived intellectual growth than do departments having other combinations of teaching and research climates.

Summary and Implications

The evidence assembled for this volume (see Table 9.1) suggests that faculty scholarship and research activity does not adversely affect faculty teaching norms, faculty teaching effectiveness, student cognitive growth and development, or professional choices made by faculty concerning the currency of course content. Moreover, most faculty and student interactions are not attenuated by faculty involvement in research. For many dimensions of teaching, faculty research activity does not adversely influence faithfulness to the ideal of service to students as clients of teaching.

However, our evidence does suggest that research activity detrimentally influences two teaching dimensions: assessment of student course performance and one facet of classroom teaching. High journal article publication productivity negatively affects the rigor of course examination questions. Heavy involvement in research also hinders the provision of prompt feedback to students, a component of good teaching practice.

These summary points have implications for expectations about the relationship between teaching and research held by the countervailing patrons of research and of teaching. The federal government as a patron holds profoundly different expectations for higher education institutions than those expectations held by state-level patrons. Federal funding for research activity is a multibillion-dollar-a-year industry in higher education that creates pressures for academic scholars to produce tangible results that justify the patron's investment—in this case, the federal government's investment. However, many state governments subsidize higher education, expecting that state funds will be used primarily to promote student learning through teaching. Both levels of government play key roles in the funding of higher education. The differing emphases valued by each set of patrons creates tension within the academy, as administrators and faculty try to fulfill their obligations to all patrons.

The unique relationship between the American professoriate, the general public, and elected public officials requires scholars to address public concerns. This need arises not only out of the ethical obligation that a professional has to a client (Goode, 1969) but also from the need to satisfy the interest of a patron in order to ensure on-going investment in the academic enterprise. The different perspectives on the relationship between teaching and research (Conflicting, Null, and Complementarity) can be viewed as a reflection of the

Table 9.1. Literature Examining the Effect of Research Activity on Dimensions of Teaching

Dimension of Teaching (authors cited)	Summary of Results
Course Content	
Braxton (1983)	Prolific scholars are more likely to require the use of scholarly books and current journal articles.
Norms as Guides to Teaching Behavior	
Braxton, Bayer, and Finkelstein (1992)	Four norms are identified.
Sullivan (Chapter Two)	Research is not harmful to teaching.
Student-Faculty Interaction	
Pascarella (1980); Sorcinelli (1991)	Faculty interaction has positive effects on students.
Bray, Braxton, and Smart (Chapter Three)	Prolific scholars are more likely to favor accessibility to students.
Olsen and Simmons (Chapter Four)	Research is not harmful to teaching.
Classroom Practices	
Braxton and Nordvall (1985)	Greater rigor of exam questions indexes higher expectations for student performance.
Braxton (1992)	
Nordvall and Braxton (forthcoming)	
Olsen and Simmons (Chapter Four)	Prolific scholars are no more inclined to emphasize personally efficient techniques than less-productive colleagues.
Johnson (Chapter Five)	Prolific scholars ask more rigorous exam questions.

Dimension of Teaching (authors cited)	Summary of Results
Effective Teaching Cohen (1981) Chickering and Gamson (1987) Sorcinelli (1991) Olson and Simmons (Chapter Four)	Course ratings are positively associated with course achievement. Six principles of effective teaching are identified. Adherence to principles of good teaching enhances student learning. Prolific scholars do not differ on five of the principles. However, they are less apt to give prompt feedback.
Student Cognitive Development Volkwein and Carbone (1994) Gavlick (Chapter Six)	Largest gains in student outcomes occur in departments that balance the emphasis between teaching and performance. Research activity may enhance certain pedagogical skills, which can result in increased student learning.
General Relationship Between Teaching and Research Braxton (Chapter One) Austin (Chapter Seven) Ludwig (Chapter Eight)	Review of previous studies shows that nineteen support the Null perspective, eleven support the Complementarity perspective, and one supports the Conflict perspective. Institutional and department culture influence how faculty members balance teaching and research. Research-Teaching emphasis mis-specifies the issues.

disparate demands placed on the academy by assorted groups of stakeholders, including the federal government and its agencies, state governments, local communities, private foundations, faculty, students, parents, and alumni. What implications do these formulations have for administrators and for institutional researchers and scholars?

Implications for Administrators

The public debate about the relationship between teaching and research presents profound implications for academic leaders and administrators. First, academic leaders and policy makers need to decide what the desired perspective is for their institution or academic department. Linked to mission and goals, this is an important, yet rarely asked, question that should be considered by administrators at all levels. Institutions and departments need to make decisions that meet the ethical obligations of the academic profession (the ideal of service), while at the same time satisfying diverse patrons. Inherent in this question is the dilemma about which perspective best fulfills the ideal of service. As neither perspective harms the client (Braxton, Chapter One), it is important for academic leaders to be intentional about, and have a strong rationale behind, the type of relationship they wish to foster between teaching and research.

Administrators are most likely to subscribe to the Null perspective when there are large discrepancies between the ways in which administrators wish to define the ideal of service and the ways in which they must meet the expectations of patrons, or even when there are dissonant expectations placed on colleges and universities from different sources of patronage. Conversely, administrators are more likely to promote the Complementarity perspective when there are higher levels of congruence between how academic leaders define their obligations toward serving clients and how they perceive their obligations to patrons. In Chapter One, Braxton notes that institutions and departments wishing to advance the Complementarity perspective will need to use specific policies and practices to buttress their efforts toward this end.

A second concern focuses on what types of policies and practices can be implemented that support the desired perspective. This volume provides a variety of policy recommendations, as follows:

- Academic leaders should confidently and publicly assert to all constituencies that teaching effectiveness and publication activity do not conflict (Braxton, Chapter One).
- Faculty, academic administrators, and presidents should engage in institutional discussions about what the nature of the teaching-research relationship should be on their campuses (Braxton, Chapter One; Austin, Chapter Seven; Ludwig, Chapter Eight).
- Faculty members must identify their values, espouse those values, and engage in behavior that reflects those values; this behavior includes appro-

priate intercession when the norms of those values are violated (Sullivan, Chapter Two).

- College and university administrators might elect to enlist the support of prolific scholars in both curricular change and in the development of policies and programs designed to encourage student-faculty contact (Bray, Braxton, and Smart, Chapter Three).
- Undergraduate students should have direct opportunities to learn from faculty about their research (Olsen and Simmons, Chapter Four).
- Academic policy makers should promote less-fragmented, more focused research activities leading to moderate scholarly production in order to emphasize teaching while maintaining research productivity (Johnson, Chapter Five).
- Shifting the balance between research and teaching roles should begin early in the professional socialization process, while future faculty are still in graduate programs (Johnson, Chapter Five).
- Institutional policy makers should assess cultural influences on the teaching-research balance at the institutional, disciplinary, and departmental levels (Austin, Chapter Seven).
- Institutional leaders must use both rhetoric and action to affect the teaching-research culture(s) on their campuses (Austin, Chapter Seven).
- Faculty seminars and colloquia, monthly bag lunches, and teaching fellows programs are needed to create conversations and networks that promote a culture in which teaching and research are both valued (Austin, Chapter Seven).
- All policies and practices should be consistent in the message they send regarding the teaching-research balance (Austin, Chapter Seven).
- Academic leaders must focus on accurately describing what faculty do, rather than merely counting how much they produce (Ludwig, Chapter Eight).

These recommendations can help administrators and policy makers gain understanding about what types of strategies will have the most impact at various levels—individual, departmental, and institutional. Most likely, a consistent combination of policies and practices designed for and aimed specifically at these three levels will be most effective in producing desired outcomes. Pascarella and Terenzini (1991) note that positive educational outcomes are most likely to occur if programmatic efforts are "broadly conceived and diverse," yet "consistent and integrated" (p. 655). More specifically, they observe that rather than any one large program, "efforts might more profitably focus on ways to embed the pursuit of that goal (in this case, either a Null or a Complementarity perspective) in *all* appropriate institutional activities" (p. 655). They suggest that the use of many small, modest policy "levers" on a regular basis is more effective in promoting a goal than using a one-time, large policy lever.

Another facet of this issue deals with ways in which institutions, departments, and individuals can be influenced toward a particular orientation. All

three levels are affected by regulatory policies, for example, assessment procedures and standards and formal reward structures (Tuckman, 1979; Centra,
1993; Fairweather, 1993). Cultural contexts—norms, beliefs, values, and
assumptions (Tierney and Rhodes, 1993; Austin, Chapter Seven)—as well as
individual faculty characteristics, that is, disciplinary affiliation (Biglan, 1973;
Braxton and Hargens, 1996), attitudes and aptitudes (Bess, 1977; Creswell,
1985), and career life cycle stages (Baldwin and Blackburn, 1981), are affected.

All of these effects must be taken into consideration when designing policies and practices as multiple policy levers meant to facilitate either the Null
or the Complementarity perspective. Taken together, multiple strategy levers
across these domains provide a powerful institutional or departmental culture
that creates a consistent frame of reference, which in turn supports the desired
goal or perspective.

Implications for Institutional Researchers and Scholars

Important and interesting questions remain for scholars interested in the relationship between teaching and research, the ideal of service, and the influence
of patronage. First, if the Null perspective is the natural condition, as Braxton
(Chapter One) asserts, then what conditions facilitate complementarity
between teaching and research? Braxton (Chapter One) speculates that individual characteristics or institutional cultures may foster complementarity
between teaching and research. Austin (Chapter Seven) articulates the importance of the impact of institutional and departmental cultures on the teaching-
research relationship. Braxton's and Austin's work suggests that future research
in this area should focus on identifying how different institutional, departmental, and individual factors affect the teaching-research relationship.

Furthermore, if there are differences between individual orientations,
departmental presses, and institutional culture on a specific campus, it is
important to know how the relationship between teaching and research is ultimately specified. In other words, the ways in which different levels (individual, departmental, institutional) affect each other need to be unpacked in a
meaningful way that creates greater understanding about how these different
forces interact to facilitate a specific type of relationship, be it null or complementarity, on a campus or in a department.

Further investigation is needed into the ways in which different disciplines
attach importance to the Null or Complementarity perspective. Given the
important differences between high- and low-consensus disciplines (Braxton
and Hargens, 1996), the natural condition for one discipline may be different
from the natural orientation of another. The research and teaching skills needed
for high-consensus disciplines may have less in common with each other than
the teaching and research skills needed for low-consensus disciplines. Hence,
complementarity may be more natural for low-consensus disciplines, and the
Null perspective may be more natural for high-consensus faculty. Socialization
may also play a key role in defining and perpetuating disciplinary preferences

for either the Null or Complementarity perspective. The training of future faculty in doctoral programs, disciplinary norms, and reward structures may all be factors that contribute to important differences between high- and low-consensus disciplines—differences that may include disciplinary pressures toward either the Null or the Complementarity perspective.

Other recommendations for research are offered in this volume, including:

- A focus on individual faculty members' behavior in specific settings is needed in order to determine how faculty members operationalize appropriate value-laden behavior and to assess how they sanction inappropriate behavior (Sullivan, Chapter Two).
- The relationship between espoused commitments to acquisition of breadth of knowledge and behavior pertinent to curricular deliberations and implementation needs to be studied (Bray, Braxton, and Smart, Chapter Three).
- A focus is needed on attitudes toward faculty accessibility to students and behavioral indices of this attitude (Bray, Braxton, and Smart, Chapter Three).
- Further examination of the influence of research activity on faculty commitment to breadth of knowledge acquisition and faculty accessibility is required (Bray, Braxton, and Smart, Chapter Three).
- The relationship between collaborative research and critical thinking questions on exams should be explored (Johnson, Chapter Five).
- The hypothesized relationships linking faculty research activity with teaching behaviors and subsequently with student achievement need to be empirically tested using path analysis or some other appropriate multivariate technique (Gavlick, Chapter Six).
- The teaching behaviors that might link research productivity and student achievement should be determined (Gavlick, Chapter Six).
- Possible mediating variables and common causes should be explored while investigating the relationship between research productivity, teaching behaviors, and student achievement (Gavlick, Chapter Six).
- More holistic descriptions of what faculty do and how they spend their time are needed (Ludwig, Chapter Eight).

Conclusion

The empirical evidence compiled for this volume strongly indicates that faculty research activity is not an intrusion on the teaching of undergraduate college students. Thus, college and university faculty warrant the public's trust in their commitment to the ideal of service to students. Nevertheless, the goals of universities and their individual faculty members need clarity so they can be communicated to stakeholders both inside and outside the academy. Given the research and policy implications described in this volume, much work remains as we attempt to further clarify the nature of academic work for ourselves and for the American public. To do less is both a violation of public trust by academic professionals and a breach of contract to public patrons.

References

Baldwin, R. G., and Blackburn, R. T. "The Academic Career as a Developmental Process: Implications for Higher Education." *Journal of Higher Education,* 1981, *52,* (6), 598– 614.

Bess, J. L. "The Motivation to Teach." *Journal of Higher Education,* 1977, *48,* (3), 243–258.

Biglan, A. "Relationships Between Subject Matter Area Characteristics and Output of University Departments." *Journal of Applied Psychology,* 1973, *57,* 204–213.

Blau, P. *Organization of Academic Work.* New York: Wiley, 1973.

Braxton, J. M. "Teaching as a Performance of Scholarly Based Course Activities: A Perspective on the Relationship between Teaching and Research." *Review of Higher Education,* 1983, *7,* 21–34.

Braxton, J. M. "The Normative Structure of Science: Social Control in the Academic Profession." In J. C. Smart (ed.), *Higher Education: Handbook of Theory and Research.* New York: Agathon Press, 1986.

Braxton, J. M. "Selectivity and Rigor in Research Universities." *The Journal of Higher Education,* 1993, *64,* 657–675.

Braxton, J. M., Bayer, A. E., and Finkelstein, M. J. "Teaching Performance Norms in Academia." *Research in Higher Education,* 1992, *33,* (5), 533–568.

Braxton, J. M., and Hargens, L. L. "Variation Among Academic Disciplines: Analytical Frameworks for Research." In J. C. Smart (ed.), *Higher Education: Handbook of Research.* Vol. 11. New York: Agathon Press, 1996.

Braxton, J. M., and Nordvall, R. C. "Selective Liberal Arts Colleges: Higher Quality or Prestige?" *Journal of Higher Education,* 1985, *56,* 538–554.

Centra, J. A. *Reflective Faculty Evaluation: Enhancing Teaching and Determining Faculty Effectiveness.* San Francisco: Jossey-Bass, 1993.

Chickering, A. W., and Gamson, Z. E. "Seven Principles for Good Practice in Undergraduate Education." *AAHE Bulletin,* 1987, *39,* 3–7.

Cohen, P. A. "Student Ratings of Instruction and Student Achievement: A Meta-Analysis of Multisection Validity Studies." *Review of Educational Research,* 1981, *51,* (3), 281–309.

Creswell, J. W. *Faculty Research Performance: Lessons from the Sciences and Social Sciences.* ASHE-ERIC Higher Education Report No. 4. Washington, D.C.: The George Washington University School of Education and Human Development, 1985.

Ewell, P. T. "The Neglected Art of Collective Responsibility: Restoring Our Links with Society." Commissioned paper for the American Association of Higher Education Forum on Faculty Roles and Rewards Second National Conference, New Orleans, January 1994.

Fairweather, J. S. "Faculty Reward Structures: Toward Institutional and Professional Homogenization." *Research in Higher Education,* 1993, *34,* (5), 603–623.

Feldman, K. A. "Research Productivity and Scholarly Accomplishment of College Teachers as Related to Their Instructional Effectiveness: A Review and Exploration." *Research in Higher Education,* 1987, *26,* 227–298.

Goode, W. J. "Community within a Community." *American Sociological Review,* 1957, 22, 194–200.

Goode, W. J. "The Theoretical Limits of Professionalization." In A. Etzioni (ed.), *The Semi-Professions and Their Organization.* New York: The Free Press, 1969.

Newman, F. "Progress Report: The University Role in Research and Technology." *Higher Education and the American Resurgence.* Princeton, N.J.: Carnegie Foundation for the Advancement of Teaching, 1985a.

Newman, F. "Researching Funding: A New Balance for Effectiveness." *Higher Education and the American Resurgence.* Princeton, N.J.: Carnegie Foundation for the Advancement of Teaching, 1985b.

Nordvall, R. C., and Braxton, J. M. "An Alternative Definition of Quality of Undergraduate Education: Toward Useable Knowledge for Improvement." *Journal of Higher Education,* forthcoming.

Pascarella, E. T. "Student-Faculty Informal Contact and College Outcomes." *Review of Educational Research,* 1980, *50,* 545–595.

Pascarella, E. T., and Terenzini, P. T. *How College Affects Students: Findings and Insights from Twenty Years of Research.* San Francisco: Jossey-Bass, 1991.

Schein, E. H. *Professional Education: Some New Directions.* New York: McGraw Hill, 1972.

Sorcinelli, M. D. "Research Findings on the Seven Principles." In A. W. Chickering and Z. F. Gamson, *Applying the Seven Principles of Good Practice in Undergraduate Education,* New Directions for Teaching and Learning, no. 47. San Francisco: Jossey-Bass, 1991.

Tierney, W. G., and Rhodes, R. A. *Enhancing Promotion, Tenure, and Beyond: Faculty Socialization as a Cultural Process,* ASHE-ERIC Higher Education Report Number 6. Washington, D.C.: The George Washington University School of Education and Human Development, 1993.

Tuckman, H. P. "The Academic Reward Structure in American Higher Education." In D. Lewis and G. Becker (eds.), *Academic Rewards in Higher Education.* Cambridge, Mass.: Ballinger, 1979.

Turner, S. P. "Forms of Patronage." In S. E. Cozzens and T. F. Gieryn (eds.), *Theories of Science in Society.* Bloomington and Indianapolis: Indiana University Press, 1990.

Volkwein, F. J., and Carbone, D. A. "The Impact of Departmental Research and Teaching Climates on Undergraduate Growth and Satisfaction." *Journal of Higher Education,* 1994, *65,* 147–167.

JOHN M. BRAXTON is associate professor of education in the Department of Educational Leadership, Peabody College, Vanderbilt University.

JOSEPH B. BERGER is a Ph.D. candidate in higher education administration, Department of Educational Leadership, Peabody College, Vanderbilt University.

INDEX

Academic cultures. *See* Cultural contexts
Action research, 74
Active learning techniques, 34, 36, 37
Adam, B. E., 31, 38
Administrative leadership, 63–64
Aguanno, J. C., 13
Ajzen, I., 27, 28
Aleamoni, L. M., 12
American Association for Higher Education, 72
Amey, M. F., 31
Angelo, T. A., 37, 38
Association of American Colleges, 2, 23, 28
Astin, A. W., 60, 63, 65
Austin, A. E., 2, 45–46, 57, 58, 59, 60, 61, 62, 65, 86, 87, 88

Baird, L. L., 61, 65
Baldwin, R. G., 45–46, 88, 90
Barry, J. L., 24
Barsi, L. M., 34, 38
Bausell, R. B., 12
Bayer, A. E., 11, 12, 15, 17, 18, 20, 24, 28, 45, 46, 80, 90
Bean, J. C., 37, 38
Becher, T., 58, 60, 65
Bensimon, E. M., 62, 65, 76
Benston, G. J., 12
Berger, J. B., 2, 79
Berquist, W. H., 58, 65
Bess, J. L., 11–12, 42, 88, 90
Biglan, A., 16, 20, 25, 28, 43, 46, 58, 65, 88, 90
Blackburn, R. T., 16, 20, 88, 90
Blau, P. M., 16, 20, 80, 90
Bloom, B. S., 42, 46
Bloom's taxonomy, 42
Boyer, E. L., 5, 12, 15, 20, 24, 28
Braunstein, D. N., 12
Braxton, J. M., 1, 5–12, 13, 15, 16, 17, 18, 20, 23, 41, 42, 43, 46, 47, 56, 58, 59, 65, 79, 80, 81, 82, 86, 87, 88, 89, 90, 91
Bray, N. J., 1, 23, 87, 89
Breadth of knowledge: as goal of undergraduate education, 23–26
Bresler, J. B., 13

Cage, M. C., 5, 13
Cameron, K. S., 59, 66
Carbone, D. A., 1, 3, 5, 14, 32, 39, 61, 62, 66, 79, 83, 91
Carnegie Classification Category, 8, 25
Carnegie Foundation for the Advancement of Teaching, 13, 25
Carpenter, C., 41–42, 47
Cates, C., 75, 76
Centra, J. A., 13, 28, 32, 42, 88, 90
Chang, M. J., 60, 63, 65
Chase, C. I., 42, 47
Chickering, A. W., 2, 3, 24, 27, 28, 34, 38, 82, 90
Clark, B. R., 5, 13, 24, 28, 58, 59, 60, 65
Clark, M. J., 13
Client Welfare: and classroom practices, 81–82; and cognitive development, 82–83; and course content, 80; and effective teaching, 82; and faculty norms, 80–81; and student-faculty interactions, 81
Cognitive development: and research activity, 82–83
Cohen, P. A., 2, 3, 49–55, 56, 82, 83, 90
Collaborative research, 45–46
Complementarity perspective: and demands of education stakeholders, 83, 86; empirical support for, 6–7; and instructional practices, 31–32, 36
Conflict perspective: and demands of education stakeholders, 83, 86; empirical support for, 6; and instructional practices, 31–35; and undergraduate education, 24
Consensus: rate of, in disciplines, 45
Contrasting perspectives: administrative implications of, 11–12, 86; assessing strength of, 8; conclusions from appraisal of support for, 8–9; implications of, for researchers and scholars, 9–11, 88–89; on relationship between teaching and research, 5–7; research support for, 7–9; support for, by institutional type, 8, 10
Corl, T. C., 58, 66
Correlation between research and student-related effectiveness of teachers, 51

Creswell, J., 43, 47, 88, 90
Critical thinking: and multidimensional role of teacher, 43–46
Cross, K. P., 37, 38
Cultural contexts: in academic field, 57–58; administrative leadership and, 63–64; assessing of, 61–62; creating networks and, 64; in departments, 60–65; in disciplines, 58–59; influence of, on policies and practices, 64; in institutions, 59–65; reward systems and, 63; and type of institution, 60
Curricular reform: administrative implications of, 27–28; defining the variables of, 25–26; faculty attitudes and, 23–28; implications of, for administration, 27–28; research implications of, 27; research procedures for, 24–26

Deal, T. E., 58, 61–62, 66
DeLorme, C. D., Jr., 14
Dent, P. L., 13
Departmental culture: and administrative leadership, 63–64; analysis of, 60–65; assessment of, 61–62; and creating networks, 64; influence of, on policies and practices, 64; overview of, 57–60; and reward systems, 63
Design inquiry model of research activity: accumulation of data in, 75–76; applied to the study of faculty, 72–74; description in, 75; reflection in, 76
Diamond, R. M., 31, 38
Dienot, E. R., 24
Disciplinary culture: analysis of, 58–59; overview of, 57–58. See also Cultural contexts
Doig, B., 41–42, 47
Doig, J. C., 41–42, 47
Drenk, D., 37, 38
Durkheim, E., 17, 20

Edison, M., 56
Endo, J. J., 33, 38
Ettington, D., 59, 66
Ewell, P. T., 1, 3, 68, 69–70, 71, 76, 79, 90
Examination item content: critical thinking questions asked in, 44; percentage of knowledge questions in, 44

Faculty: accessibility of, to students, 25–27; accountability of, 69; and disci-

plinary consensus, 17–18, 26, 43, 45; ideal of service, 79, 89; publication productivity of, 15–20, 43; responsibility of, 67–68; work of, 68–72
Faculty scholarship. See Research activity
Faculty-student contact, 24, 28, 32–33, 35, 36, 37, 81
Faia, M. A., 6, 7, 13, 32, 38, 63, 66
Fairweather, J. S., 31, 32, 38, 63, 66, 88, 90
Faver, C. A., 45, 47
Feldhusen, J. F., 14
Feldman, K. A., 2, 3, 7, 8, 13, 31, 32, 33, 38, 47, 49–55, 56, 59, 66, 82–83, 90
Finkelstein, M. J., 6, 7, 13, 15, 16, 17, 18, 20, 80, 90
Fishbein, M., 27, 28
Fox, M. F., 1, 3, 6, 13, 45, 47
Freedman, K. A., 13
Frey, P. W., 13
Friedrich, R. J., 13, 32
Fulton, O., 24, 28
Funding of higher education: roles of different levels of government in, 83

Gaff, J. G., 23, 24, 26, 28
Gamson, Z. E., 2, 3, 24, 27, 34, 38, 82, 90
Gavlich, M., 2, 49, 82, 83, 89
Geertz, C., 57, 66
Gill, J. I., 75, 76, 77
Gmelch, W. H., 34, 38
Goldner, J., 6, 13
Goode, W. J., 20, 31, 38, 79, 80, 83, 90
Gordon, G. G., 43, 47, 58, 66
Gronlund, N. E., 42, 47
Guthrie, D. S., 24, 28

Hagedorn, L., 56
Hargens, L. L., 16, 17, 20, 58, 65, 88, 90
Harpel, R. L., 33, 38
Harry, J., 6, 13
Head Start, 68
Hedges, L., 13
Hicks, R. A., 13
Higher Education Act (1992), 68
Hoffman, R. A., 13
Hoyt, D. P., 13
Hutchings, P., 74, 76

Institutional culture: analysis of, 59–65; assessment of, 61–62; and curricular reform, 23; and departmental culture, 58; impact on undergraduate experience, 32

Integrity in the College Curriculum, 23
Intellectual self-discipline of teacher, 54
Jacobs, L. C., 42, 47
Jakubauskas, E. B., 13
Johnson, R. M., Jr., 2, 41, 81, 87, 89
Jones, P., 59, 66

Kendall, P. L., 15, 20
Kennedy, A. A., 58, 61–62, 66
Kerr, C., 5, 13, 24, 28
Kingsolver, B., 73, 74, 76
Kirshstein, R., 6, 13, 24, 28, 29
Kratwohl, D. R., 42, 47
Kuh, G. D., 57, 58, 59, 66
Kuhn, T. S., 43, 47

Lawrence, J. H., 16, 20
Layzell, D. T., 69, 71, 72–73, 75, 77
Lee, F. D., 37, 38
Levine, D., 68
Lewis, D. J., 13
Liebert, R. J., 24, 28
Light, R., 7, 13
Light, W., Jr., 58, 66
Likert scale, 25
Linsky, A. S., 6, 7, 13, 16, 20
Lodahl, J. B., 43, 47, 58, 66
Lord, F. M., 42, 47
Lovell, C. D., 77
Loverich, N. P., 34, 38
Ludwig, M. J., 2, 67, 77, 79, 86, 87, 89

McClelland, D., 47
McCullagh, R. D., 14
McDaniel, E. D., 14
McGann, A. F., 13
Madus, G. F., 42, 47
Magoon, J., 12
Marquardt, R. A., 13
Marsden, L. R., 58, 66
Marsh, H. W., 14
Massy, W. F., 1, 3, 5, 14, 23, 28, 32, 38, 69, 77
Merton, R. K., 15, 20, 31, 38
Mets, L. A., 59, 66
Michalak, S. J., Jr., 13, 32
Moore, K. M., 31, 38
Moore, W. E., 15–16, 20
Morstain, B. R., 24, 29
Murray, H. G., 14

Narrative type of research evidence, 73
National Center for Educational Statistics, 35, 38

National Survey of Postsecondary Faculty, 69
New Directions for Institutional Research, 1, 67
Newman, F., 80, 90
Nobel Prize, 70–71
Nora, A., 33, 39, 56
Nordvall, R. C., 41, 42, 43, 46, 47, 81, 90, 91
Null perspective: of relationship between teaching and research, 6, 8, 9, 83, 86
Nuttal, R. L., 42

Olkin, L., 13
Olsen, D., 2, 31, 33, 38, 81, 82, 87
Orenstein, A., 68, 77
Overall, J. W., 14

Palmer, P. J., 64, 66
Paradigm development, 58–59, 73, 74
Parsons, T., 6, 13, 24, 28, 29
Pascarella, E. T., 33, 39, 41, 55, 56, 81, 82, 87, 91
Paunonen, S. V., 14
Payne, D. A., 42, 47
Peters, R., 69, 73, 77
Peterson, M. W., 57–58, 59, 62, 66
Platt, G. M., 6, 7, 14, 24, 28, 29
Platt, J. R., 14
Policy–relevant research. *See* Public policy debate on faculty
Portch, S. R., 68, 77
Pratt, A. M., 68, 71, 77
ProfScam: Professors and the Demise of Higher Education (Sykes), 69
Proscriptive norms. *See* Teaching norms
Public: expectations of, 5; and lack of understanding for academic research, 68; misperceptions of, 12, 68–72; as patrons of research, 79–80
Public policy debate on faculty: responsibility of those engaged in, 74; the role of research in the framing of, 67–76; and social control over faculty role performance, 79–80
Publication productivity: analysis of, 43–44; implications of, for policy and practice, 19; levels of, 43; measures of, 18, 43–44; relationship of, to inadequate planning, 17–18; relationship of, to interpersonal disregard, 17–18; relationship of, to moral turpitude, 17–18; relationship of, to particularistic grading, 17–18; and teaching norms, 15–20

Quinlan, K. M., 24, 29

Rate of article publication, 44–45
Rate of book publication, 44–45
Rating-achievement correlations, 52, 53
Reader, G. G., 1, 20
Reiss, A., 16, 20
Research activity: analyzing the variables of, 26; and choice of instructional practices, 31–38; and cognitive complexity of student examination questions, 41–46; cultural context of, 57–65; defining variables of, 25–26; effect of, on dimensions of teaching, 84–85; and faculty attitudes supporting undergraduate curriculum reform, 23–28; and faculty culture, 23; influence of, on teaching norms, 15–20; and instructor effectiveness, 5–12, 50; and meeting educational needs of students, 79–89; obtaining data about 25; role of, in framing public policy debate, 67–76; and specialization, 23; and student achievement, 49–56
Research evidence, types of, 73
Research I institutions, 17, 34, 35, 41, 45
Research II institutions, 41, 45
Reward systems, 63. See also Cultural contexts
Rhodes, R. A., 31, 38, 88, 91
Riordan, T., 71–72, 77
Rokeach, M., 27, 29
Role conflict theories, 31
Roskens, R., 43, 47
Roy, M. R., 14
Ruscio, K. P., 55, 56, 59, 66
Rushton, J. P., 14

Saunders, L., 73, 75, 76, 77
Scheffe, 35
Schein, E. H., 58, 66, 80, 91
Scholarly consensus: in departments, 58–59; influence of, on conflicting perspectives, 16–18
Scholarship Reconsidered: Priorities of the Professoriate (Boyer), 5, 24
Schon, D. A., 71, 72, 73–74, 76, 77
"Seven Principles for Good Practice in Undergraduate Education: Faculty Inventory" (Chickering, Gamson, and Barsi), 24, 27, 34
Shils, E., 6, 14
Sieber, S. D., 32, 36, 38

Siegfried, J. J., 14
Simmons, A., 2, 31, 33, 38, 81, 82, 87
Singhal, S., 14
Smart, J. C., 1, 23, 24, 29, 45, 46, 87, 89
Smith, P., 7, 13
Sorcinelli, M. D., 81, 82, 91
Spangler, R. K., 13
Spencer, M. G., 57–58, 62
Springer, L., 33, 39
Stallings, W. M., 14
Stark, J. S., 24, 29
Stavridis, P. G., 14
Stewart, A. A., 47
Straus, M. A., 6, 7, 13, 16, 20
Student achievement, 49–56, 82–83
Student-faculty interactions, 24, 81
Student-rated teacher effectiveness, 51
Students: as clients, 79–89, cognitive development of, 82–83
Study Group of the Conditions of Excellence in American Higher Education, 15, 20
Stumpf, S. A., 13
Sullivan, A. V. S., 1, 15–20, 80–81, 86–87, 89
Sykes, C. J., 69, 77

Teachers: instructional effectiveness of, as measured by student achievement, 50–53; intellectual self-discipline of, 54; multidimensional role of, 42; subject knowledge of, 54; workloads of, 24
Teaching: determining essence of, 71; effectiveness of, 49–56; instructional dimensions of, 32; normative control structures of, 15–20; role conflicts in, 15
Teaching evaluation process: broadening of, 37
Teaching norms: and client welfare, 80–81; as control structures, 15–20, 80; and inadequate planning, 17–18; and interpersonal disregard, 17–18; and moral turpitude, 17–18; and personal disregard, 17–18; and publication productivity
Terenzini, P. T., 33, 38, 39, 41, 47, 82, 87, 91
Thoits, P. A., 32, 39
Thoreau, H. D., 74
"Thoughts from the First Forum on Faculty Roles and Rewards" (Change), 31, 39
Tierney, W. G., 23, 29, 66, 88, 91

Toombs, W., 23, 29, 41, 47
Trow, M., 24, 28
Tuckman, H. P., 88, 91
Turner, S. P., 79–80, 91

Undergraduate education: research activity and, 23–28
U. S. Congress, 75
U. S. Department of Education, 68, 77
Usher, R. H., 9, 10, 14

Veysey, L. R., 5, 14, 24, 29
Voeks, V. W., 7, 14
Volkwein, F. J., 1, 3, 5, 14, 32, 39, 61, 62, 66, 79, 83, 91

Wasescha, A., 26, 28
White, K. J., 14
Whitt, E. J., 57, 58, 59, 66

Wilger, A. K., 32, 38
Wilke, P. K., 34, 38
Wilson, R. C., 24, 29, 72
Wingspread Good Practices subscales, 34–37
Winkler, A. M., 77
Winston, G. C., 31, 39, 68–69, 77
Winter, D., 47
Wolfle, L. M., 55, 56
Wood, L., 24
Wood, N. J., 14
Wood, P. H., 14
Woods, E. M., 42
Wright, T., 33

Yimer, M., 12

Zemsky, R., 1, 3, 5, 14, 23, 28, 69, 77
Zuckerman, H. E., 20

ORDERING INFORMATION

NEW DIRECTIONS FOR INSTITUTIONAL RESEARCH is a series of paperback books that provides planners and administrators in all types of academic institutions with guidelines in such areas as resource coordination, information analysis, program evaluation, and institutional management. Books in the series are published quarterly in spring, summer, fall, and winter and are available for purchase by subscription as well as by single copy.

SUBSCRIPTIONS for 1996 cost $50.00 for individuals (a savings of 34 percent over single-copy prices) and $72.00 for institutions, agencies, and libraries. Please do not send institutional checks for personal subscriptions. Standing orders are accepted.

SINGLE COPIES cost $19.00 plus shipping (see below) when payment accompanies order. California, New Jersey, New York, and Washington, D.C., residents please include appropriate sales tax. Canadian residents add GST and any local taxes. Billed orders will be charged shipping and handling. No billed shipments to post office boxes. Orders from outside the United States or Canada *must be prepaid* in U.S. dollars or charged to VISA, MasterCard, or American Express.

SHIPPING (SINGLE COPIES ONLY): $10.00 and under, add $2.50; $10.01–$20, add $3.50; $20.01–$50, add $4.50; $50.01–$75, add $5.50; $75.01–$100, add $6.50; $100.01–$150, add $7.50; over $150, add $8.50. Outside of North America, please add $15.00 per book for priority shipment.

DISCOUNTS FOR QUANTITY ORDERS are available. Please write to the address below for information.

ALL ORDERS must include either the name of an individual or an official purchase order number. Please submit your order as follows:
   Subscriptions: specify series and year subscription is to begin
   Single copies: include individual title code (such as IR78)

MAIL ALL ORDERS TO:
   Jossey-Bass Publishers
   350 Sansome Street
   San Francisco, CA 94104-1342

FOR SUBSCRIPTION SALES OUTSIDE OF THE UNITED STATES, CONTACT:
any international subscription agency or Jossey-Bass directly.

OTHER TITLES AVAILABLE IN THE
NEW DIRECTIONS FOR INSTITUTIONAL RESEARCH SERIES
J. Fredericks Volkwein, Editor-in-Chief

IR89 Inter-Institutional Data Exchange: When to Do It, What to Look for, and How to Make It Work, *James F. Trainer*
IR88 Evaluating and Responding to College Guidebooks and Rankings, *R. Dan Walleri, Marsha K. Moss*
IR87 Student Tracking: New Techniques, New Demands, *Peter T. Ewell*
IR86 Using Academic Program Review, *Robert J. Barak, Lisa A. Mets*
IR85 Preparing for the Information Needs of the Twenty-First Century, *Timothy R. Sanford*
IR84 Providing Useful Information for Deans and Department Chairs, *Mary K. Kinnick*
IR83 Analyzing Faculty Workload, *Jon. F. Wergin*
IR82 Using Performance Indicators to Guide Strategic Decision Making, *Victor M. H. Borden, Trudy W. Banta*
IR81 Studying Diversity in Higher Education, *Daryl G. Smith, Lisa E. Wolf, Thomas Levitan*
IR80 Increasing Graduate Student Retention and Degree Attainment, *Leonard L. Baird*
IR79 Managing with Scarce Resources, *William B. Simpson*
IR78 Pursuit of Quality in Higher Education: Case Studies in Total Quality Management, *Deborah J. Teeter, G. Gregory Lozier*
IR77 Developing Executive Information Systems for Higher Education, *Robert H. Glover, Marsha V. Krotseng*
IR76 Developing Effective Policy Analysis in Higher Education, *Judith I. Gill, Laura Saunders*
IR75 Containing Costs and Improving Productivity in Higher Education, *Carol S. Hollins*
IR74 Monitoring and Assessing Intercollegiate Athletics, *Bruce I. Mallette, Richard D. Howard*
IR73 Ethics and Standards in Institutional Research, *Michael E. Schiltz*
IR72 Using Qualitative Methods in Institutional Research, *David M. Fetterman*
IR71 Total Quality Management in Higher Education, *Lawrence A. Sherr, Deborah J. Teeter*
IR70 Evaluating Student Recruitment and Retention Programs, *Don Hossler*
IR69 Using National Data Bases, *Charles S. Lenth*
IR68 Assessing Academic Climates and Cultures, *William G. Tierney*
IR67 Adapting Strategic Planning to Campus Realities, *Frank A. Schmidtlein, Toby H. Milton*
IR66 Organizing Effective Institutional Research Offices, *Jennifer B. Presley*
IR65 The Effect of Assessment on Minority Student Participation, *Michael T. Nettles*
IR64 Enhancing Information Use in Decision Making, *Peter T. Ewell*
IR61 Planning and Managing Higher Education Facilities, *Harvey H. Kaiser*
IR60 Alumni Research: Methods and Applications, *Gerlinda S. Melchiori*
IR59 Implementing Outcomes Assessment: Promise and Perils, *Trudy W. Banta*
IR58 Applying Statistics in Institutional Research, *Bernard D. Yancey*
IR56 Evaluating Administrative Services and Programs, *Jon F. Wergin, Larry A. Braskamp*
IR55 Managing Information in Higher Education, *E. Michael Staman*
IR47 Assessing Educational Outcomes, *Peter T. Ewell*
IR39 Applying Methods and Techniques of Futures Research, *James L. Morrison, William L. Renfro, Wayne I. Boucher*
IR37 Using Research for Strategic Planning, *Norman P. Uhl*
IR36 Studying Student Attrition, *Ernest T. Pascarella*